THREE RINGLINGS IN MONTANA

THREE RINGLINGS IN MONTANA

Circus Trains to Cattle Ranches

Lee Rostad

RIVERBEND PUBLISHING

Three Ringlings in Montana
Text © 2015 by Lee Rostad

Published by Riverbend Publishing, Helena, Montana

ISBN 978-1-60639-078-8

Printed in the United States of America.

2 3 4 5 6 7 8 9 0 VP 22 21 20 19 18 17 16 15

Cover design by Sarah Cauble, www.sarahcauble.com
Text design by Barbara Fifer

Photo credits
Front cover: A steam locomotive pulling a stock train on John Ringling's White Sulphur Springs and Yellowstone Park Railway, 1940. (Ron V. Nixon Collection, RVN10833, Museum of the Rockies, Montana State University, Bozeman, Montana)
Back cover: Painting of a steer head by western artist Charles M. Russell for logo of the Bozeman Roundup, an annual rodeo supported by Richard Ringling.
(Courtesy of Laura Potter McMillan)
Daring Madam Castello on the equine marvel Jupiter, from a Ringling Brothers Circus poster, circa 1899.

Riverbend Publishing
P.O. Box 5833
Helena, MT 59604
1-866-787-2363
www.riverbendpublishing.com

CONTENTS

RINGLING, MONTANA

THE RAILROAD NO LONGER runs through the town of Ringling, Montana; the bank is gone; the hardware store and livery are gone. A closed church and school remain, along with a number of houses. Only the bar/restaurant and the post office remain to service the few resident families and surrounding ranchers. There are only the memories of when the bustling town welcomed homesteaders and other settlers. There is nothing left of the railroad that John Ringling built except the ruins of the depot.

So, the people of Ringling were surprised in the fall of 2006 to have PETA (People for the Ethical Treatment of Animals) ask them to change their name back to the original "Leader."

"The name Ringling conjures up in people's minds images of elephants being beaten with bull hooks and tigers being crammed into tiny cages..." said Rae-Leann Smith. Smith was the specialist in circus issues for PETA in Chicago. "And we think it's a shame for the nice people of Ringling to be associated with that animal cruelty."

As an inducement to the townspeople, PETA offered an incentive—$15,000 worth of "hearty and humane" veggie burgers for the Meagher County School District.

The ranching community said, "No, thanks."

This faded newspaper photo shows the two-sides-open lion cage of Ringling Brothers Circus's 1897 season.

During the Ringling Brothers and Barnum & Bailey Circus 1922 parade from the railroad into Philipsburg, Montana, a Keystone Kop clown "races" to catch up to his assigned position.

PREFACE

THE CIRCUS COMES TO MONTANA

THE FIRST RINGLING BROTHERS CIRCUS performance in Montana took place in Dillon, on May 31, 1897.

The circus trains began pulling into the station in four distinct sections, carrying in total nearly 100 railroad cars of circus performers, ticket takers, accountants, trapeze artists, and roustabouts—the workers who set up and took down the tents—as well as traveling stock: the lions, tigers, bears, elephants, and horses.

Imagine the looks on the faces of the townspeople as the circus folks began unloading: elephants swinging their trunks as they plodded down the ramps from the boxcars, the tigers snarling in their horse-drawn cages, the clowns with their painted faces and bright suits, the ringmaster who resembled an orchestra conductor with his dark suit and baton and commanding presence. The Ringling Brothers Circus paraded through town from the railroad station to the fairgrounds, trailed by a growing crowd of townspeople.

That year the circus also appeared in Anaconda, Butte, Helena, Great Falls and Havre. En route from Butte to Helena, it encountered a problem. A Great Northern train crew came

TO GET THE TRAIN UP OUT OF BUTTE HEADING NORTH, ONE ENGINE PULLED AND ONE ENGINE PUSHED

near not getting anywhere because an elephant drank the water in the tank on the engine coal car.

It was the first section of the Ringling circus. The train started for Helena with one engine in front and one behind. The climb out of Butte over the mountains toward Helena is a heavy drag all the way up hill. One engine alone couldn't pull the train nor could one alone push it. In fact, the two engines had all they could do to get the train up out of Butte, and were nearly stalled in tunnel No. 10. The engines were burning Sand Coulee coal, and the smoke and gas in the tunnel was nearly enough to kill both men and animals.

Otto Bjornstad, fireman on the train (and later a Great Falls city jailer), had a helper on the engine tender pushing coal down to the fireman. They had just gotten through the tunnel, when there was a crash in the car next to the head engine. An elephant in the car had pushed out its end door. Then the beast stuck its trunk through the opening, lifted the lid off the water tank and started to drink. As the water level fell in the tank,the steam pressure in the engine went down. There was very little water left. The train stopped and Bjornstad climbed back over the coal to make the elephant quit drinking, but its wavering trunk limited his efforts to vocal ones.

Crew members tried to cut the engine loose from the train but the elephant's waving trunk rendered it impossible for anyone to get within reach of the coupling. The water was getting low, however, and it was imperative that they do something, so they disconnected the cars behind the elephant's, took elephant and front-of-train along to Woodville to replenish the water supply. The diminished supply gave out just as they reached there.

At Woodville the elephant wouldn't let anyone near enough to the tank to fill it. After fussing awhile, members of the train crew discovered a man sleeping in the elephant car. It was the animal's keeper. They wakened him, and the thirsty pachyderm backed up. The tank was filled and the engine went back to the train.

Entries from the Ringlings' route book give us scattered pictures of the railroad circuses in Montana in the early 1900s, as well as a glimpse of the life underneath the Big Top. The Ringling Route Book of 1900 portrays the intensity and difficulty of the travel that the performers, workmen, and animals endured as they were "trouping." As the circus pulled into Great Falls in August 20, 1900, the route book portrays the mixture of travel and rites of passage that occurred in the midst of a season. The circus "traveled all day yesterday and last night. Fred Lamont and Miss Belle

Carmen were married here tonight. Mr. and Mrs. Leon were present. It rained hard after the day show." In Great Falls, western artist Charlie Russell enjoyed meeting the circus people, and delighted them with gifts of his sketches.

The next day, they had packed up and arrived in Helena, by the "forenoon."

> Charles E. Nixon, former dramatic critic of the Chicago Inter-Ocean, has just started a newspaper here.
> The news of the wedding is spreading today and Fred Lamont is busy shaking hands.

A day later, on Wednesday, August 22, the troupe was in Bozeman, nervously entertaining more American Indians. "The Indians are getting more numerous. They were well represented here."

In Butte, the next day, the record shows that

> Marks was left last night in Bozeman. He climbed on the first train that came to town and instead of coming here he went back to Helena. "Jig Steps" was also left. Tonight the boys had some fun with a fresh laundry-man. He pulled a revolver in the dressing room and they took it away from him.

By Friday, August 24, they had arrived in Anaconda, and the journal keeper noted "Marcus Daly owns this town. It is very chilly today and we are wearing our overcoats."

In Missoula for Saturday, the journal keeper noted the presence of numbers of Indians, with some trepidation.

The Indians have come from miles around to see the show. Their tents were pitched on the lot when we arrived. We gave only an afternoon show here.[1]

The circus easily encountered bad weather in Montana. On September 4, 1902, they even encountered a sandstorm in Butte, when:

small particles of dirt and stone were dashed into the eyes and faces of workingmen and many of them were almost blinded…As the circus commenced, swirling dust was so thick in the big top that all the chandeliers were lighted and even the persons on the seats could scarcely discern the actors. The storm continued all day and late into the night, and everybody, from the Ringlings to the smallest pony boy, was glad when Butte was in the distance.[2]

1. *The Circus: A Route Book of Ringling Bros. World's Greatest Show*, Season 1900 (Chicago: Central Printing and Engraving, 1900).
2. *The Circus*, 24.

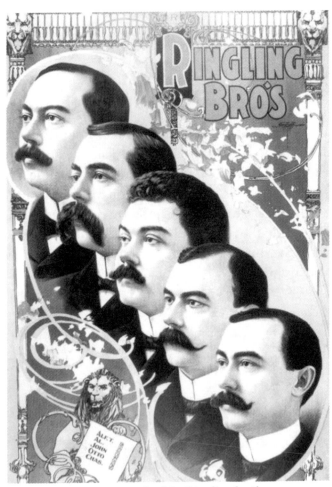

The circus program portrait of the Ringling brothers

THE GREATEST SHOW ON EARTH

FIVE RINGLING BROTHERS

THE RINGLING BROTHERS CIRCUS was founded in 1884 by John Ringling and his four brothers, Albert (called Al), Alfred Theodore (known as Alf T.), Otto, and Charles. They were five of the seven surviving sons and one daughter born to August and Marie Rüngling.

August had come to the United States when he was twenty-one years old. He changed the spelling to Ringling, and married Marie Salome Juliar in 1852 in Milwaukee. They lived in Chicago and

Milwaukee before settling in Baraboo, Wisconsin.

Albert was their first son, born in 1852, followed by August, Otto, Alfred, Charles, John, Henry and the sole daughter, Ida, who was born in 1874. When August senior's business failed in 1858, he moved his family to McGregor, Iowa, where the boys watched steamboats, barges and fur boats coming and going along the Mississippi River. Circus companies and other traveling shows were the main forms of entertainment—and the Ringling boys witnessed the fanfare and color of those that arrived in McGregor by steamboat.

As their nephew Henry Ringling North recalled in *The Circus Kings: Our Ringling Family Story,* the Ringling boys had permission to go in the early morning to await arrival of Dan Rice's "Brilliant Combination of Arenic Attractions." Along with the steamer's lights coming up the Mississippi, Alf T. recalled the music and color of the circus arriving in town.

The old river calliope made music that was sweet. All its sharpness and its terror were mellowed as it passed over the water, and by the time it reached the shore it was as soft and soothing as a cradle song.

The boys watched as red and gold chariots were unloaded from the accompanying barge, were harnessed to the horses, and, with drivers aboard, started for the show grounds. The scene, with the bright chariots and the exotic animals, must have been dream-like.

The carved and gilded chariots were eased carefully off, as their teams were simultaneously brought off the main boat and hitched up with the precision of a well drilled battery of horse artillery. Then came the animals—a nose-ringed bear or two, a grumpy camel, the white broad-backed horses of the equestrians, and finally the elephant, testing the gangplank with probing trunk and one great forefoot. Iron-gray, the color of sky and water, he was monstrously magnified by the mist.[1]

"RINGLING CIRCUS ADMISSION 5 CENTS" WAS THE BROTHERS' VERY FIRST ADVERTISING

Entranced, the five Ringling brothers decided to start their own show. Their first circus was held in a "pavilion" made of scraps of canvas, old carpets, and moth-eaten army blankets. Alf said they charged an entrance fee of one penny and the show netted $8.37 that was promptly put back into the show by the purchase of muslin sheeting for a sizable tent.

The first show circus, as North described in *The Circus Kings*, was "announced" to the town of McGregor starting with a parade featuring a fife, mouth-harp, bugle, harmonica, and beating drum, which of course attracted townspeople to their porches, then to the street. Al Ringling led playing the bugle, while his four brothers, wearing plumes as well, made up the band. They were followed by a small boy carrying a sign—five-year-old John Ringling—announcing the circus.

In the parade marched a motley crew of clowns and a flatbed "Democrat wagon" painted in gaudy reds and yellows, and drawn by a desiccated black mustang pony, with "superb harness by A. Ringling" and a red, white, and blue sheep's-wool plume nodding from his head.

Otto Ringling came next, leading a battle-scarred goat known locally as Billy Rainbow. Otto renamed and retrained the goat as a "hippo-capra." As the youngsters knew they would, McGregor followed the Ringlings to the vacant lot where their circular tent was pitched. From its center pole, a young pine tree cut from the nearby woods, floated an American flag and homemade pennants. Over the entrance was a sign that read: RINGLING CIRCUS / Admission 5 cents.

Despite the steep admission, more than one hundred townspeople of all ages lined up to give their money to Otto, in order to stare at the grand entry, known professionally as "Spec. Alf T., King of the Sandwich Islands." He was dressed in an old Union officer's dress uniform, a cape made from a crazy quilt, and a gilt paper crown, and rode the pony. He was followed by the band and the performers, now dressed in tights made of long winter underwear dyed gaudy colors and meagerly bespangled and decorated with fancy ribbons. Last came the goat again, Billy Rainbow, now led by five-year-old John Ringling.

Just as the crowd was probably wondering if they were really getting their five cents' worth, the King of the "Sandwhich" Islands dismounted and bowed, and Billy Rainbow broke loose and butted him in the seat of his pants. Al juggled plates, laughter growing with each plate he broke, following by a tumbling act and clown song, "Root, Hog, or Die." Charles Ringling appeared riding on a mustang on a saddle devised from blankets and a cellar door, and each time he mounted the horse, it bucked him off. North concluded that it was his Uncle Albert who "bellwethered" his four brothers into a life of showmanship although the others were willing followers.[2]

Although John began his career singing and dancing, in maturity he took on the role of route overseer. A dashing man who married his wife after they had been in a car accident and she'd prayed for his survival. When he was pulled from the wreck, he announced, "That's the girl for me!" After John convinced his brothers to convert from travel wagons to rail cars in the 1880s, "he became a human encyclopedia on road and local conditions," according to the *New York Times*.[3]

In 1884, the Ringling Brothers Circus was founded in Baraboo, and the company returned there each winter after touring the country. The town became known locally as "Ringlingville." The Ringling brothers built a structure along the Baraboo River that, from 1897 through 1916, was the largest circus structure in North America, and is today a National Historic Landmark Site. In 1907, the brothers bought the Barnum & Bailey Circus and ran it separately until merging the two in 1919 into Ringling Brothers and Barnum & Bailey Circus: The Greatest Show on Earth! The circus grew from a small operation to one of the three largest circuses in America, employing more than one thousand people.

THE YEAR 1919 SAW THE BEGINNING OF RINGLING BROTHERS AND BARNUM & BAILEY CIRCUS

In Baraboo after the circus season until 1927 (when winter quarters moved permanently to Sarasota, Florida), the brothers improved their acts, costumes and exhibits. They endured the trials of wagon, then rail travel, shows that had to be canceled, and rail-union strikes. Initially, each of the five had his own specialty. Charles was in charge of moving the army of people and animals through months of one-night stands. Otto was financial manager. Alf T. was in charge of public relations and, according to John Ringling North, used all the

> means and media which stimulated an overwhelming desire to see the circus in everybody within one hundred miles or so of any town where the show was playing.

This was important in those years of the "circus wars," when many circus companies were fighting for audiences. Gus was the advance man and Henry worked at "the front door." The signature photo for the circus advertising, in 1888, showed only Albert and Otto with mustaches, but by 1891 all five were sporting mustaches. They used this photo until Otto's unexpected death in 1911.

The circus's first few years were difficult. Albert had worked for Fayette Lodawick "Yankee" Robinson, a well known circus man, and he persuaded the veteran to come with the Ringlings. With his drawing power, the brothers posted the show as "Yankee Robinson and Ringling Bros. Great Double Shows, Circus and Caravan," the only time any billing put another's name ahead of the Ringlings'. When Yankee died in 1884, the Ringling brothers were on their own. They put on 241 "hall shows" (indoor performances) in Illinois, Wisconsin and Iowa before returning to Baraboo.

EACH YEAR BROUGHT NEW ACTS AND SPECTACLES, AND THE BIG TOP GREW LARGER

Each year, the brothers added something new to their show. In 1887, the main tent was a ninety-foot round top, accompanied by a thirty-foot round top, a sideshow tent forty-five by fifty-five feet, and the menagerie in a seventy-foot round top. They had sixty horses and five cages of wild animals. They moved the circus hundreds of miles with horse-drawn wagons over rough, rutted roads. They put up the tents each morning, put on a parade and show, took down the tents and moved on to the next spot. In the winter, they sent out hall shows to augment the income.

A year later, the circus had two elephants, two camels, three lions, a hyena, deer, kangaroo, zebras, emu, birds, monkeys and eighty head of horses and ponies. They doubled the admission from 25 cents to fifty.

In 1890, when Charles Ringling married, his wife Edith embraced the circus life, beginning as a ticket seller. Charles's death in 1926 did not stop her, and then she also became active on the board. In her private railcar, she traveled with the company until the 1950s. Often called "Mrs. Charlie," she attended nearly every performance.

These circus visits were set into motion weeks ahead of time by John Ringling, the advance man, who traveled ahead to schedule the circus site, ticket sales, and advertising. Described as an "impeccably dressed man" who was "tall, with curly hair and droopy eyes," he was an expert on where railroads ran and who ran each one.[3]

When the circus started traveling by rail, they traveled in four squadrons or sections carrying a total of fifteen hundred people and a thousand animals from town to town.

The company traveled by train until 1956, when it switched to trucks. Paul Ringling, Richard's son and Alf T.'s grandson, recalled that the circus used teams and elephants, "plus some old 1917 Mack trucks to move all the wagons and everything" up until 1980. Whichever mode had gotten them to the day's location, the circus moved with 4-, 6-, and 8-horse teams of horses, mostly Percherons, particularly grays, so there were, in Paul's words, "lots of beautiful big gray horses."[4]

To move a circus from place to place—to organize setting up and taking down and then transporting people, equipment, and animals—required tremendous effort, timing, and planning. When the country was preparing for World War I, the army studied the Ringlings' movement methods. The *Baraboo Weekly News* of May 23, 1912, reported that two officers spent two weeks traveling with the show. The mission, the report noted, was to

> study the methods by which a circus moves so smoothly and rapidly. It has been estimated that taking into consideration the total number of people with the circus, nearly 1,300, and the fact that it carries about 1,000 animals and 650 horses, besides all the necessities of a moving village, the machinery of the thing must be worth observation. No army detachments in action has ever pitched camp and moved each day with such rapidity.

BEFORE ENTERING WORLD WAR I, THE ARMY STUDIED HOW THE RINGLING BROTHERS CIRCUS MOVED SO EFFICIENTLY AND QUICKLY FROM TOWN TO TOWN

When Ringling Brothers was smaller, its circus train consisted of two advertising cars, one performers' sleeper, one elephant car, five stockcars, and eight flatcars—eighteen cars in all. These transported two tableau wagons, two band wagons, fifteen cages (four open dens included) and one hundred and seven horses, three elephants, three camels, four lions, two cub lions, a hippopotamus, and assorted other wild creatures, besides fifty-four performers. However magnificent it was compared with the little wagon show that had started so hopefully out from Baraboo six years before, it was still only a one-ring show, peanut-sized compared with the great railroad shows it was about to challenge.

As Paul recalled in a 2013 interview,

> …by this time the circus in America had reached a high state of development. Phineas T. Barnum, the greatest showman of them all, had hurled himself into the circus business with a tremendous splash in 1872, when my uncles were holding their five-cent circus. By 1873, eleven years before the Ringling wagon show started, Barnum's *Advance Courier* could describe his circus as a "Colossal World's Fair by Railroad."[5]

After the Ringlings enlarged their circus to four trains, it meant that John had to plan the exact time of each section every day, in cooperation with many railroads and branch lines. Paul outlined how it worked.

> The circus had four trains—four sections, four trains. The circus owned all of its own railroad stock but contracted with different railroads to move the trains. The engines and engineers, and brakemen, they worked for whatever railroad you happened to be on. But the circus owned its own rolling stock.

• • •

Each section, Paul noted, contained specific parts of the circus that related to the overall layout. The first section, that left at 9:30 P.M., contained the cookhouse layout and as many as fifty elephants. The second section that left at midnight contained the Big Top, or large canvas tent, as well as the big top crew and ushers. The third section left later in the night carrying the side shows, the freaks, the tattoo lady, the fat man, the thin man, the giant, the pin head, the snake charmer and hula dancers.

THE CIRCUS HAD ITS OWN ROLLING STOCK OF RAILCARS——ENOUGH TO MAKE UP FOUR TRAINS

The fourth and final train was the sleeping section that included the actors and trapeze artists, as well as the stock train that was, according to Paul, "72 cars long." The stock included work horses, performing horses, zebras, lions, tigers, and monkeys.

Through the Depression years, John continued to have problems managing the circus's and, later, his own finances.

The Ringling Circus had traditionally opened the season at Madison Square Garden. New management had changed the terms of the usual Ringling circus contract for a month's engagement in the spring of 1930. The rent was increased, but more importantly a key clause permitting the circus to have uninterrupted use of the arena was deleted.

Ringling's friend and associate Tex Rickard had died and William Carey, the new manager, insisted on reserving Friday evening each week for the Garden's professional boxing—more profitable for the Garden than the circus. Ringling was outraged, and rejected the new agreement.

When he refused to sign, the same contract was at once offered to the American Circus Corporation's Sells-Floto and Hagenbeck–Tom Mix combined show, who accepted immediately. Since Ringling could not buy the contract for the Ringling Circus, John made a deal with the American Circus Corporation to buy the circuses. He bought the entire operation, including five circuses, equipment, show names, and quarters in Peru, Indiana, and Denver, Colorado for $2 million. In the name of the Ringling Circus, he borrowed $1.7 million and gave his personal guarantee for the note. The purchase came only days before the stock market crash, which stopped him from his plan to charter a public corporation and to market the shares. On the personal side, in February he also lost his yacht *Zalophus* in the Gulf of Mexico.

John's wife Mable died in New York in the early summer of 1929 from diabetes and Addison's disease. The loss of his mate of twenty-five years was devastating. Mable had been by his side as he collected art from Europe and planned the museum that would be the home of their vast art collection. Built at a cost of $1.5 million, Ca'd'Zan is still a premier art museum in Sarasota.

Feeling the loss of Mable, Ringling remarried to Emily Hauk Buck, a young socialite he had met in Europe. It was not a successful marriage, adding to John Ringling's problems.

Tent circuses flourished until the Great Depression, but in 1931, circus attendance was down so much that the show closed September 14, the earliest closing in its long history.

John's biographer, David C. Weeks, summed up the circus man's position:

At the center of Ringling's problems was the Prudence Bond Company and its two subsidiaries: New York Investors and Allied Owner. In 1929, when Ringling was searching for funds to purchase the American Circus Corporation, William Greve, the central figure of this network, suffered to advance the needed funds. The hand of Sam Gumpertz was not in evidence at this point, but he was intimately associated with the group. The circus purchase price was $2 million. Ringling found about $300,000 in cash, most of it from another loan. Greve arranged for the Central Hanover Trust Company of New York to advance the $1.7 million on a personal promissory note signed by John Ringling, endorsed by the New York Investors. Later, Allied Owner purchased the note from the bank without Ringling's knowledge. In consequence, New York Investors, as the parent company, acquired an interest in the loan. That note ran for only six months, unsecured by any Ringling collateral. Ringling, trusting in Sam Gumpertz (who had introduced him to these financiers), believed he was among friends.[6]

DURING THE GREAT DEPRESSION, JOHN RINGLING PILED UP DEBTS FOR CIRCUS AND PERSONAL NEEDS

In ordinary times, the purchase of the American Circus Corporation would have made sense, but with the Depression's advent, Ringling was juggling his assets and, when he could not meet payments, he fell deeper into debt. In the spring of 1932, he signed away his personal assets.

But he didn't stop spending the company's or his own seeming fortune.

When John Ringling was forced to sign away his assets, his wife Emily urged him not to agree to their demands, which she rightly believed would leave him broke. She tried without success to bring in an attorney whom she trusted. Emily perceived, as John did not, that Kelley, the circus attorney, was pushing the interests of the circus as he saw them and that he was supporting Edith Ringling. Emily saw clearly that John Ringling was without an ally within the circus. For too long he had plunged ahead, indifferent to his partners and brushing aside all who questioned his total command.

The one concession John demanded and got, was that another corporation be formed called the Rembrandt Corporation, to which he deeded his art collection. He then put up the stock of his corporation as part of the collateral his creditors demanded.[7]

The Delaware corporation received one-tenth of the stock: John, Edith, and Aubrey would each receive a third of the rest. The $1,017,000 debt was assumed by the corporation and secured by John's personal assets.[8]

At the next shareholders' meeting, Gumpertz took control. Although the other shareholders (Edith, Aubrey, and the creditors) did elect John president, they made it clear they named him only to a titular post. Gumpertz, as general manager, would run the company, and Edith and Aubrey would serve as vice presidents.

John Ringling voted his 30 per cent of the stock against the proposition. Edith voted her 30 per cent for it; Gumpertz's group voted their 10 per cent of the stock in his favor, so the balloting stood 40 per cent for, 30 per cent against. At this, Aubrey said there had been enough votes cast so she would not vote.

John focused his bulldog eyes on her. He would spare neither her nor himself. According to John Ringling North, "You will vote, Aubrey," he said. "I must know where you stand."

When John Ringling continued to recruit new circus talent, Gumpertz ordered him to stop. John's health was failing, and soon he was no longer to participate in the great circus he and his brothers had founded.

In 1932, John Ringling suffered a coronary thrombosis and was confined to a wheel chair. He died four years later.

World War II Years

Dissension came again in 1943. The Norths wanted to "wait out the war" with the circus. It was impossible to get fire retardant tents. To fight any fire, the circus tent was surrounded by water trucks and pumps and "able bodied young men." However, during the war, able bodied men were hard to find. In most years the circus employed 1,600 and in 1942, had 1,200.

North proposed that the circus operate on a non-profit basis for the duration of the war and perform for military installations and USOs, trusting that the government would give them priority in having fire retardant supplies and transportation. North presented the plan to the board. Edith, her son Robert, and Richard's widow Aubrey voted to continue the circus. North immediately resigned and Robert Ringling took over circus management.

The big fire came in Hartford, Connecticut, during an afternoon show in July of 1944. Within minutes, the paraffin-coated tent was a flaming mass, and at least 168 people died. Given the apparent lack of proper fire control, the police arrested six circus officials for involuntary manslaughter. Robert was in New York at the dentist that day, but James Haley had been on the grounds. He, along with the other five officials, was sentenced to a year and a day. The circus agreed to pay death and injury claims from future earnings and, by 1950, had paid out $3.9 million.

Robert did not fight for Haley in court and did not visit or write to Haley in prison. Haley felt he had "taken the fall" for Robert and he and Aubrey shifted their support to John Ringling North.

By 1947, Robert North had suffered a stroke and was no longer interested in the family feud.

Aubrey finally became weary of the fighting. Both she and husband James Haley sold their stock. The sale of the Haley stock amounted to 140 shares to John for $194,444.48; 175 shares to Robert for $24,055.55. This left John Ringling North with an accumulated total of 510 shares and Robert and Edith with 490.

Aubrey and James walked away with $437,500.[9]

In 1967, the last of the Ringling heirs sold the circus out of the family.

The Ringling family in about 1895. Standing, left to right: Al, Alf T., Gus, Charles, and Otto. Seated, John, mother Marie, father August, Ida, and Henry. COURTESY OF WISCONSIN HISTORICAL SOCIETY, WHS-56729

1. Henry Ringling North and Alden Hatch. *The Circus Kings* (Garden City, NY: Doubleday & Company, 1960).
2. *Circus Kings*.
3. Jerry Apps, *Ringlingville USA: The Stupendous Story of Seven Siblings and Their Stunning Circus Success* (Madison: Wisconsin Historical Society Press, 2005), 24.
4. David Lewis Hammarstrom, *Big Top Boss: John Ringling North and the Circus* (Urbana: University of Illinois Press), 24.
5. Paul Ringling interview by Caroline Patterson in March 2013.
6. David C. Weeks, *Ringling: The Florida Years, 1911-1930* (Gainesville: University of Florida Press, 1993), 234-5.
7. Weeks, 236.
8. *Big Top Boss*, 31.
9. *Big Top Boss*, 122.

The long-ago train station...and its train-car exhibit

RESORT AND SUPPLY CENTER

WHITE SULPHUR SPRINGS

JAMES BREWER HAD SETTLED at the west-central Montana Territory hot springs in 1866, putting up a dirt-roofed log shack, and building a log stable and a log bathing room. There were thirteen springs in the area. Brewer used the water of two of them for the bath house, and fixed one up for drinking, but apparently never filed on the water rights. He tried for ten years to create a resort, borrowing money to operate.

His creditors foreclosed and the property was

sold at sheriff's sale in 1876. It was bought by Dr. William Parberry.

According to the diary of Almon Spencer (1838-1909), which he kept all of his life:

> The Springs Hotel at that time consisted of a long, low, dirt roofed log building, with the family living quarters in the front, next a room for transient guests, next a room for a small stock of store goods and post office, (newly transferred from Diamond City). The ornate new Springs Hotel just being built, a two-story log building with office, dining room and twenty-six bedrooms, was a really swell establishment for that day. Dr. Parberry, who had come from Diamond City in 1877, had a dirt roofed log building just north of the row of log buildings and this was where he and Mrs. Parberry lived.[1]

Dr. Parberry was at that time a prominent man in his community, a member of the territorial council in 1879, member of the constitutional convention and Democrat senator from Meagher County to the first state legislature.

He was born in Bourbon County, Kentucky, in 1833. His parents were of Scotch-Irish descent through old colonial stock. Two forebears won fame in the Revolutionary War and his father took part in the Battle of the Thames, 1813, when Tecumseh was killed.

His parents moved to Kentucky from Virginia in 1826 and, since they died when he was but a lad, he had few educational advantages. He was one of those who are hungry for knowledge, and he studied by firelight after his hard day of work until he was able to teach school. He taught at Jefferson City, Missouri, and immediately began the study of medicine. He took a course of lectures at St. Louis Medical College in 1856, and was graduated from Jefferson Medical College, Philadelphia, in 1858, and after returning to Missouri and practicing there for six years he entered Bellevue Hospital Medical College.

In 1865 he came to Montana, locating at Diamond City. He married Matilda Hampton, daughter of Hannah and Cynthia (Mitchell) Hampton of North Carolina, in 1872.

Dr. Parberry was a real factor in the town's growth and served as assessor, commissioner and treasurer. He was president of the First National

JOHN RINGLING PURCHASED THE PARBERRY MANSION, AND LATER SOLD IT TO RICHARD RINGLING

Bank and, when he retired from business, he owned a stock ranch of 15,000 acres in Sweet Grass County.

The Parberrys eventually built a house at the lower end of Main Street, an imposing residence for its time. It was later purchased by John Ringling, who sold it to his nephew Richard for one dollar in 1918. Richard maintained it as his family's Montana home.

In 1878 another Diamond City settler moved to White Sulphur Springs. Jonas Higgins had bought a drove of mules in Indiana and started them for Montana in 1865. Many of them died in Wisconsin and many more were stolen in an Indian raid on Diamond City. But Mr. Higgins took the proceeds of his venture and bought a stock of merchandise. He maintained the store at Diamond City until 1878, when he moved his stock to White Sulphur Springs.

There was no strife or rivalry whatever between Parberry

and Higgins at first. Neither had yet acquired title to his property and it is doubtful whether the land had yet been surveyed. It was understood that when platted the main street would follow "the main traveled stage road between Fort Logan and Martinsdale." This main road went north, east and south to go around the swampy area of the springs.

Upon the strength of this supposition, Higgins built his store building upon the "main traveled road." He erected it in 1879 and it was the first real store, although goods had always been kept by the Springs Hotel proprietors.

Dr. Parberry, about this time, began to entertain different views as to where the main street of the future town should be located and was not blind to how his property value would be enhanced if it had an approach from the west, with the main street running between his hotel and the springs and bath houses. To this end he constructed a corduroy road west, and as soon as he had obtained patent to his land he had it surveyed, platted and presented to the board of county commissioners. It became the original town site of White Sulphur Springs, with the main street located as it is today, leaving Higgins' new store building stranded and lonely about 150 or 200 feet back from the street.

DR. PARBERRY BOUGHT THE HOT SPRINGS AND PLATTED THE TOWNSITE

This infuriated Higgins and he swore he would plat his own town site and not conform his streets to the Parberry plan. This he proceeded to do. He had his town site platted, presented it to the county commissioners for approval, and they accepted the plat and permitted it to be filed.

Their consent was not given in ignorance of the storm the matter was arousing among partisans of one or other of the antagonists. Probably the commissioners were quite sincerely troubled about the best course to pursue. The *Rocky Mountain Husbandman* of that period comments dryly that "the commissioners held another mum sociable last night" and did nothing. Had they refused to accept Higgins' plat, there would have been nothing for him to do but to have his land resurveyed and make his streets and alleys conform to the original town site. "Had they had a vestige of business judgment or vision, they would have done so," says one who remembers the fight,

but they were not business men. They were three old ranchers, friends of both Parberry and Higgins, reluctant to take sides either for or against either party in what seemed to them only a personal quarrel, and by their colossal blunder they became officially responsible for the egregious situation.

The town continued to grow. A school was established in 1878, and in 1880 Gideon Spencer built a store. In Almon Spencer's words,

In the early eighties settlers began coming to the valley, and, in just a very few years the entire valley was settled, the store did a flourishing business...In the year 1882 and for many years thereafter the business was conducted under the firm name and style of Spencer Mayn & Heitman....newcomers to the community were astonished to find, instead of a roistering, gun-toting element, a community of quiet, intelligent, peace loving people...In 1882 several new business buildings were put up on Main Street, and a few small residential buildings began to spring up.

On upper Main Street someone put up a feed stable and still farther up, the red light distinct was located. The rear end of the stable building was large enough to furnish quarters for a saloon of the dive type.

The valley settled up rapidly, the population of the town increased for a few years, and the town became an important supply point, being the only supply point within a radius of from fifty to one-hundred miles in different directions.

Being so far away from railroad, freighting became a major problem and a major occupation...

When my father built the store, Fort Benton was the logical wholesale supply point for the territory, on account of the cheap water transportation up the Missouri river from Bismarck. From there it was hauled to various points in the territory by "Bull team", horse team or mule team. It was one-hundred-eighty miles to Fort Benton, and the round trip took anywhere from three to four weeks, according to the weather conditions.

...During the years 1880-82, my father had the freight ha[u]led from Ft. Benton at a cost of three cents per pound: in the year 1883 the Northern Pacific Railroad was completed as far as Livingston, Montana, a distance of seventy-five miles from White Sulphur, and the freight was hauled by team from there for a year or two at a cost of seventy-five cents per hundred, then the railroad reached Townsend, a distance of forty miles from W.S.S. and the freight was hauled from there for twenty-five years at a cost of forty cents per hundred.

Then when the Milwaukee railroad was built through Montana, a station was located at Dorsey, a distance of twenty miles, from where freight was hauled in for twenty cents per hundred.

Dr. Parberry sold his townsite with all the remaining unsold lots and his other town property to the White Sulphur Springs Association, a corporation formed by capitalists from Helena and other Montana cities for the purpose of improving and advertising the hot springs as a health resort. Spencer wrote:

At that time everyone expected the town to become a place of importance and predicted that the association would be s successful institution, but the town was off the sidelines, the expected railroad never materialized, the town never grew, and the White Sulphur Springs Association gradually faded away, reached a point where it couldn't even pay the taxes, fell into the hands of the Merchants National Bank of Helena which failed in 1893, and finally fell into the hands of the Conrad-Stanford Company of Great Falls, and remained in a moribund condition for many years.

Then, in the early 1900s, John Ringling, one of the richest men in America, became involved in White Sulphur Springs.

1. Almon Spencer, diary, Meagher County Historical Society, White Sulphur Springs, Montana.

Detail from portrait of John Ringling by Savely Sorine

THE "BEST MILLIONAIRE," FLAMBOYANT CIRCUS MAN & ART COLLECTOR

JOHN RINGLING (1866—1936)

As HE TRAVELED AROUND America in the early 1900s, John's job was to keep the Ringling Brothers Circus appearances scheduled. The day-to-day business was done by his brothers Alfred, "Alf T." and Charles. John, a businessman with a talent for making money, he always had his eyes out for a business opportunity—whether a failing movie theater that needed some propping up, or a steam laundry that needed an influx of cash to get back into the black. As a developer, he would buy up acreage, form a land company, and then resell tracts to farmers or ranchers moving into the area.

John made investments across the circus's path: Oklahoma oil fields or Florida land at Sarasota, and he helped build a new Madison Square Garden in New York City. By 1903, *Fortune* magazine ranked him the "best millionaire alive," because of his sartorial flair, Fifth Avenue mansion, Venetian palazzo in Sarasota, and the *Wisconsin*, his private railroad car.[1]

His favorite investment seems to have been short-line rail systems. When he spotted a missing link in the rail system, he saw an opportunity for profit. About 1911, he built a line between Mark Twain's home town of Hannibal, Missouri, and Bowling Green, Kentucky, and gave it the grandiose title of the "St. Louis and Hannibal" line, although it went nowhere near St. Louis. Another short line was a twenty-mile stretch in Texas. When he was teased about the length of that one, John assured his critics that although it was a short stretch, it was just as wide as any other. A railroad he built in Oklahoma did not succeed, but when oil was discovered underground, he became a wealthy man.

When John passed through Montana in the early 1900s, he spotted ranch land near White Sulphur Springs, a Montana "hot spot," and spied the potential for a railroad spur between the town of Leader and White Sulphur Springs.

JOHN RINGLING INVESTS IN MONTANA

Lloyd Penwell, a Montana promoter from Helena, had steered the investment-minded John to Meagher County in west-central Montana.

First, in 1903, John purchased Catlin Land and Livestock—20,000 acres of land with 2,000 of them in hay and timothy. The herd was choice Hereford beef stock. Penwell also suggested that John look into building a spur railroad between White Sulphur Springs and the Montana Railroad.

In 1907, Ringling bought 70,000 acres more in the Smith River Valley and with William L. White of New York formed the development company of Ringling and White, Inc. (This company included "control" of 30,000 more acres.) They put out a booklet regaling farmers with the great opportunities in agriculture from running dairy cattle, turkeys, sheep, hogs, poultry to crop farming, suggesting peas that could be canned and shipped. Directors of the company were Lewis Penwell,

John Ringling—dapper with cane and hat—in Sarasota

John Ringling, R.M. Calkins, Jr., R.M. Hodgens, H.H. Pigott, T.H. Vivian, C.B. Witter. They ran ads weekly in the local paper advertising

> 100,000 acres of land for sale in the famous Smith River Valley—Large and small tracts for sale on easy terms—Town Lots in White Sulphur Springs, Buy Early Before the Rush...

There was a further inducement for

> "...bona fide farmers to buy the land[.] Ringling & White, Inc. will build all or any buildings and improvements required by the purchaser, changing only actual cost, or they will sell the settler lumber and material at wholesale prices to build themselves. Live-stock and equipment will also be furnished at reduced prices.

The booklet also assured the farmer that there would be support in finding markets and furnishing agricultural advice.

> By operating farms in the section on his own account, Mr. Ringling has learned that many crops can be grown successfully and at a profit. His own farm is stocked with the best registered cattle, and he is a large owner of hogs and sheep.

The venture did not immediately take off. Instead, many newcomers took advantage of the Homestead Act. The Free Homestead Act of 1862 entitled anyone who filed to a quar-

ter-section of land (160 acres). It was necessary for the applicant to "prove up," which meant the applicant lived on the
land for five years. One could also live on the land for six
months and buy the land for $1.25 an acre. The Desert Land
Act of 1877 gave 640 acres to any claimant who irrigated the
land within three years. The person had to pay 25 cents per
acre up front and an additional amount later.

JOHN RINGLING & THE SULPHUR SPRINGS

On May 2, 1910 the editor of the *Meagher Republican* reported that John Ringling of the "Ringling Brothers Circus
people" had purchased the Springs property of the "Conrad-Stanford interest" and planned to build a $200,000 bath-
house and hotel. The editor also reported that Ringling, a
stickler for high quality, had verified that of the hot water.

Mr. Ringling sent a German chemist here from Baden-
Baden, Germany, for the purpose of analyzing the waters of which so much had been heard, and his report to
his employers was that the thermal waters of White Sulphur Springs possessed such high degree of virtue that
it is doubtful whether better springs can be found on the
Western hemisphere, and that the location and general
health conditions of White Sulphur Springs were such
as would eminently lend itself to the development of a
health resort.

As a result, John Ringling communicated with Lewis Penwell, a banker in Helena, who asked that townspeople and
residents of the Smith River Valley amass an investment of
$50,000 for the enterprise. The advent of a depressed econ-

omy dashed Ringling's plans for an elaborate renovation of the White Sulphur Springs resort.

John Ringling's Railroad

At the turn of the century, White Sulphur Springs needed a railroad. Sutherlin, in the *Rocky Mountain Husbandman*, repeatedly called for a railroad through Meagher County that could make White Sulphur Springs "the greatest city of health and pleasure in the Rocky Mountain Northwest." He went on to imagine the benefits trains could bring to the area.

Our mines of coal, lead, copper and gold and possibly silver, will come to the front and an era of prosperity inaugurated never before approached. Let us swing our hats, give three loud lusty cheers and beat the tom-toms until the welkin ring with joy for the day of our deliverance from the lumbering stage coaches and pokey freight teams.[4]

To spur growth, the town fathers (White Sulphur Springs Association) had long hoped for a railroad to come up the North Fork of the Musselshell but it never materialized. From businessman Almon Spencer's lifelong diary comes a history of their experiences:

Ever since the early settlers of our town and valley established themselves, they seemed to have some justification for the thought that a railroad would come our way. The Northern Pacific Railroad was approaching from the east, and the shortest and most direct line from Glendive to Helena could not help but come thru White

Sulphur. But it did miss us, going through by Livingston, Bozeman and Townsend to Helena. For nearly thirty years following that time, our town was languishing through the lack of railroad facilities, but we still clung eagerly to every forlorn hope.

Finally the Milwaukee Railroad starting building towards the West, and as it became nearer, we were sure that it would have to come up the North Fork of the Musselshell and down the North Fork of Smith River, and couldn't possibly miss our town. But it did miss it. It came up the South Fork of the Musselshell and down Sixteen Mile Creek on the track of the old Jawbone Railroad, and connected with the Northern Pacific at Lombard. The nearest it came to us was at Dorsey station eighteen miles south of our town. Another hope blasted—and this was our last chance. Now there was nothing to do but try to get the Milwaukee to build a branch into our town, but they were not interested. Now we were up against it. We had to have a railroad. (So we thought). And if we couldn't get it any other way we would have to build it ourselves. It could have been built very cheaply, down the South Fork of Smith river on a water grade, no bridges, no grades, no cuts: the rails and ties could have been laid practically on top of the ground. (Oh, if we had only known what we learned to our sorrow later, we wouldn't have been so frantic for a railroad, as some of the local freight rates on the branch line were higher than the wagon freight had been)....

Lewis Penwell, of Helena, had been a very successful promoter of land deals for a few years prior to this time, and he busted himself trying to get John Ringling to build a branch line from Dorsey into our town.[3]

With his record of building small railroads across the country, and with the continued urging of the association, John Ringling eventually agreed to build a railroad to White Sulphur Springs. The route, which did have a much more level grade than the Jawbone, followed the south fork of the Smith River and was laid around small hills and river valleys. As Sutherlin, the editor of the *Rocky Mountain Husbandman*, pointed out, "With a railroad to our town and proper bath and hotel accommodations, there is no reason why we should not have a town of ten thousand inhabitants in a few years....White Sulphur Springs now passes out of history as one of the most prominent inland towns of the West, and from this time forward will begin to take on Metropolitan airs." Headlines read, "Railroad! After 20 years of waiting Famous Old Town sees Hopes Consummated. Residents have given themselves over to a big jollification."

Incorporation papers were filed in June 1910 for a railroad to run from White Sulphur Springs south to the northern boundary of Yellowstone Park, a distance of approximately 125 miles. There was also a provision that the railroad could be extended northwest to Great Falls, but the immediate goal was to connect with the main Milwaukee Railway at Dorsey. Stock worth $300,000 was issued, 51 per cent given to the Milwaukee Railway as payment for materials and 49 per cent to Ringling to pay for construction costs. Work began almost immediately; by fall, the rail line for White Sulphur Springs & Yellowstone Park Railroad was laid to Dorsey.

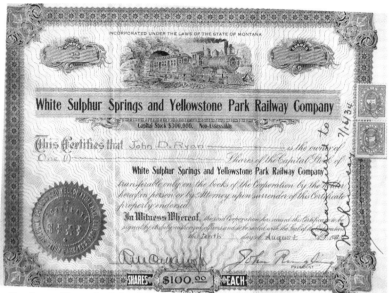

INCORPORATED UNDER THE LAWS OF THE STATE OF MONTANA

White Sulphur Springs and Yellowstone Park Railway Company

Capital Stock $300,000. Non-Assessable

This Certifies that John D. Ryan — is the owner of One (1) — Shares of the Capital Stock of

White Sulphur Springs and Yellowstone Park Railway Company transferable only on the books of the Corporation by the holder hereof in person or by Attorney upon surrender of this Certificate properly endorsed

In Witness Whereof, the said Corporation has caused this Certificate to be signed by its duly authorized officers and to be sealed with the Seal of the Corporation this tenth day of August A.D. 192

PRESIDENT

SHARES $100.00 EACH

Stock certificate for John Ringling's grandly named railroad.

The laying of track spawned a flurry of plans for new buildings, a grand hotel, Odd Fellows Temple, Episcopal Church, and houses. The town of Leader, near Dorsey, changed its name to Ringling in appreciation of the railroad. When the Milwaukee moved its line though Ringling, they leased the track from Ringling to Dorsey to the White Sulphur Springs & Yellowstone Park Railroad, which extended the line one mile further. The Milwaukee Railway also leased rolling stock to the new railroad, which included an engine, several freight cars, passenger cars, and a snow flanger.

Not everyone saw the railroad as a success. Almon Spencer gives a detailed account of the railroad episode, a story he called "dismal":

This is how John Ringling "built the railroad"—first, he directed that the town raise fifty thousand dollars by popular subscription towards the enterprise, and then he would put up the balance of the money necessary to build and equip the railroad. This the town proceeded to do, though it was vastly more than was necessary to build the kind of railroad he built.

Our store and bank headed the list with a subscription of fifteen hundred dollars, the other store and bank, as I remember it, put in little or nothing.

Under high-pressure methods every business house in the town was solicited to contribute all they could afford—and more, and then every individual citizen in the town and valley was practically forced to sign up for all they could and in this way the goal was reached—or nearly so. So the railroad was assured. The money was to be paid when the railroad was completed.

(To be perfectly frank I will say that when it came time to collect the money it fell short of fifty thousand dollars, and, if my memory serves me right there was only about thirty-five thousand actually collected; because, in getting the subscriptions a number of people who had signed up for one hundred or two hundred dollars were not financially responsible for that many cents, and the bonus fell short to that extent.

Whatever the amount, it was a straight out gift to Ringling, as all that he was out was for labor and the railroad ties; the Milwaukee R.R. furnished the rails, which were old second hand used material, and it furnished the equipment consisting of an old broken down engine and an old caboose.

So the railroad was built and equipped, and who owned it no one in our town knew, but the general supposition was that it was owned jointly by Ringling and the Milwaukee.

THE SMITH RIVER DEVELOPMENT COMPANY

When the railroad was built in 1910, The Smith River Development Company was formed with Lewis Penwell, John Ringling, R.M. Calkins, Jr., R. M. Hodgens, H.H. Pigott, T.H. Vivian and C.B. Witter. It was capitalized at $1,000,000. Again from Spencer:

Now, as a part of the general scheme of which the R.R. was only a part, they wanted to acquire all the largest ranches in the valley, and, to that end, Penwell and Ringling organized a corporation which was called the Smith River Development Company, with a capital of fifty thousand dollars, I think, although it may have been one hundred thousand.

They were to buy up all the large ranches on time and the money derived from the Smith River Development Co. was to be used to make the initial payment on the loans. I don't know how much money they derived from the Development Co., but I do know that neither Penwell or Ringling put very much, if any, into it. Neither do I know much about who any of the other subscribers were, but I do know that E.J. Anderson and I put in ten thousand dollars—five thousand each.

We entered late this enterprise very reluctantly, as we had our belly full of the land business by that time, but it seemed that we almost had to do it. We had a store

and a bank in the town depending on popular patron-
age, and there was an outfit that was buying up almost
all the land in the alley and building a railroad into the
town. What else could we do? We wanted to have the
good will of such powerful interests—certainly didn't
want to incur their ill will at the start. But we entered
into it with many misgivings, which subsequent events
warranted.

Well, they were off to a flying start. The Smith River
Development Company bought up all the ranches they
could, something over one hundred thousand acres,
at prices that ranged from six to eight dollars per acre,
using the money put up by the suckers who invested
in the Smith River Devel. Company to make the initial
payments. They established offices in the town. It was to
be a grand colonization scheme. Ringling and Penwell
were to bring in trainloads of people who would buy up
these six and eight dollar lands, at twenty-five to fifty
dollars per acre, and the Smith River Devel. Co. was
going to make a fabulous fortune.

But as soon as they got started, if the Penwell outfit
made a deal, the Ringling bunch would spike the deal,
and vice versa. The result was that they went along
for about a year, until the next installment payment
was due on their land contracts, and by that time the
Smith River Devel. Co. was broke and couldn't meet
the payments. They had no credit and couldn't borrow
any money, but at that time T.L Belseker, a large land
operator from North Dakota agreed with the Penwell
office to buy the Catlin Ranch of Twenty-Two thousand
acres at seven dollars per acre cash. This would have

given them something over one hundred forty Thousand dollars, and would have enabled them to meet all their impending payments, but Ringling refused to concede to this, and made the counter proposal that he would put up enough money to meet all their impending payments, but if he did, the company would have to assign all their contracts to him. This was a characteristic Ringling maneuver…and they had to dance to his music. This settled the Smith River Development Company. They were a hopelessly bankrupt concern, and were only a name.

SMITH RIVER DEVELOPMENT COMPANY WENT FROM OWNING 100,000 ACRES TO BANKRUPTCY

They had bought the land at very cheap prices, but they had been compelled to assign all their contracts to Ringling, and he now owned all the land at their original cheap price minus the amounts that had been paid down on the initial payments. In other words he owned some of the best ranches in Smith River Valley at prices of not much over five dollars per acre, and the Smith River Development Company was broke, and the poor suckers who had put their good money into it could take it out in gnashing their teeth.

The town built the railroad and Ringling and the Milwaukee owned it. The Smith River Devel. Co. made the initial payments on one hundred thousand acres of cheap land, and Ringling owned the land.

Now as to E.J. Anderson and G.K. Spencer, we fed the kitty of the Smith River Devel. Co. to the extent of ten thousand dollars, and it landed in the capacious maw of John Ringling. Besides about two thousand five hundred dollars that our store and bank had contributed to the railroad bonus, which landed in the same place

But to continue the tale of woe, down to the very depths of its irony, the ten thousand dollars we contributed to the Smith River Devel. Co. fell on barren soil. The railroad outlaws and the Ringling Ranch brigands gave their store and ranch business very largely to the other bank and store. We contributed more in money and influence than anyone else, and all we got was the crumbs from the table.

Obviously, Almon Spencer was not a fan of John Ringling. He wrote:

There were CROOKS and CROOKS and there was JOHN RINGLING. It had been my misfortune to have been pitted against crooks during all the years since I had grown up to manhood but to the above named personage, I will give credit for being the master minded crook of the ages.

In the fall of 1910 Smith River Development had purchased the Catlin ranch outright (on a contract) and obtained the right to purchase the Mayn and Heitman ranches at some point in the future provided they kept up the payments on the option. It appears that Ringling loaned the SRD Co. $16,000 (to obtain this option) at eight percent interest, due in the spring. Increasing Ringling's security position on the $16,000 loan, SRD assigned Ringling the option contract for the Mayn and Heitman ranches. The SRD Co. made only one payment on the note.

Ringling bought the Mayn and Heitman ranches and continued to add other ranches to his personal properties, plus the right of way for the railroad and a number of plots in the Ringling and White Sulphur area from the Northern Pacific Railway. By 1913, Ringling had 69,404 acres, according to Meagher County tax records.

Ringling maintained a real estate office in the Springs with R.M. Calkins as manager, handling land sales, hay, grain and farm products, but also dealt in sheep, cattle and horses for the local ranchers. He also managed a small number of reconditioned railroad cars, used in Yellowstone Park. His aim was to help promote the supports of the agricultural industry.

At least during the rainy years of the 1910s, John's efforts helped some of the farmers, as more wheat resulted in the building of a grain elevator in Ringling. On October 15, 1915, the *Meagher County Republican* detailed the happy news:

> An elevator here has been an imperative need to the town and community and it is through the efforts of Joseph Muggli and the State Bank that capital was secured for the project. The bank here deserves all the credit for the success of the plan, and for its activity in working for the best interests of Ringling.

THE END OF THE RAILROAD

The Ringling railroad had difficult times from the beginning. The people at Calkins (a stop that was several miles outside of White Sulphur Springs) complained because there was neither a railway platform nor a depot at their

THREE RINGLINGS IN MONTANA

stop. Cream that was being shipped out, and feed coming in, sat out in the sun and the wind. When they wrote John Ringling about the situation, the owners of the Smith River Valley Mercantile Company of Calkins also reported that when several land-seekers from Nebraska got off the train, they stepped into two feet of mud and water.

Weather also contributed to the problems. When Ringling asked Superintendent A.J. Nicholson for a report on a 1911 derailment, Nicholson explained the cause:

The matter of the derailment of which you speak... was occasioned by a broken rail in the Dorsey cut on January 23rd, engine 54 was derailed and partly turned over necessitating the use of steam derrick to rerail her.[4]

This, however, was just the beginning of the story. The train crew had met a lot of heavy snow, and when they reached this particular cut at Dorsey, the crew increased the speed of the train to make a run for it. About 100 feet into the drift the engine left the rails and partly turned over, breaking the pilot and the snow plow. In February 1911, another blizzard delayed the train's getting from White Sulphur Springs to Ringling—from Wednesday morning until Saturday afternoon. Another time, the train was tied up in snow between Moss Agate and Dorsey. The story of the train, bound in heavy snow between towns, was repeated over many winters.

In 1914, runs were reduced to three times a week, but passengers complained about the layover, and the daily mixed train was reinstated. Although many passengers traveled the short line, the mixed train was used unless a special occasion warranted a regular passenger run.

Although the railroad only conducted approximately 15,000 tons of freight business, it kept running partly because of it was managed very economically. When the train crew wasn't running the train, they doubled as section crew, and maintained bridges and track. Nevertheless, the railroad struggled as business decreased in the 1920s. A stock dividend was paid in 1921 and then there were no dividends until 1936. Freight tonnage fell to 6,700 tons in 1932.

WSS&YPRR OPERATION WAS TROUBLED FROM THE BEGINNING

In spring 1941, Ringling contacted W.C. Ramsey at the Ringling Railroad in Hannibal, Missouri, to ask him if he would run the Montana line. Instead, Ramsey sent George Wetherell, a young man of twenty-one. When George and Gladys arrived in White Sulphur Springs, they stayed with Richard and Aubrey Ringling until they could find lodging. Soon they became an active part of the White Sulphur Springs community, and close friends of the Ringling family. Their daughter, Kay, remembered that there were always free circus tickets when the circus played in Montana.

Throughout the 1940s, the line prospered, carrying carloads of wood, stock, sheep, wheat wool, farm machinery, highway material, and general freight. The railroad spur was running when the lumber business arrived in White Sulphur Springs in the 1940s, and soon shipments of lumber were added to shipments of livestock. But the tracks were in disrepair and the roadbed was rough, and the railroad repair truck could often be seen on the nearby highway accompanying the train in order to put the engine back on the rails when it wandered. In the community, talk of abandonment was again in the air.

By 1944, the railroad had only a few thousand dollars left in the corporation owned by the Milwaukee Railway, which had begun abandonment proceedings. Area stockmen and residents were firmly opposed to abandonment. By December 1944, George Wetherell of White Sulphur Springs and W.C. Ramsay of Hannibal, Missouri, acquired the Milwaukee's interest. Wetherell bought the stock owned by Ramsay, and he and John Ringling North became major stockholders. Wetherell knew that passengers had complained about sharing the train with cargo, so in 1944, he and his wife went to Hannibal and bought an old bus. They brought it back to Montana and transformed it to run on the rails. It soon became known as the "Galloping Goose."

A BUS CONVERTED TO RUN ON THE RAILS SOON WAS NICKNAMED THE "GALLOPING GOOSE"

In 1975, the line was plucked from its deathbed by King Wilson, an oil man from California, who purchased the line for a tourist attraction. He brought an old steam engine from the hills of Virginia. He also bought a day car and a bar car that he renovated in a very elegant, Victorian style. The train was to be only a part of a return to the nostalgic past with plans for a village with a blacksmith shop, a school (for dances), a bakery, general store and an opera house. He took the car out on a few excursions—but it was difficult to get the engine steamed up properly, and tourists didn't materialize in great enough number to make the venture a success.

The railway achieved its fifteen minutes of fame when the producers of the film *Heartland* shot the White Sulphur Springs & Yellowstone Park Railroad in White Sulphur Springs. The movie tells the story of Elinore Pruitt Stewart, a solo woman homesteader whose letters written from April 1909 to November 1913 formed the basis of the film.

FROM WHITE SULPHUR SPRINGS TO SARASOTA: TAYLOR GORDON AND JOHN RINGLING

When John Ringling came to town in his private car with several couples from the East, along with Mr. and Mrs. L.N. Scott of St. Paul, Fred Loomas of Chicago and the Wardens of Joliet, Illinois, and Mr. and Mrs. Allen, he hired young Emmanuel Taylor Gordon to be his driver.

Taylor Gordon, who grew up in White Sulphur Springs and went on to become a concert tenor, singing in Europe for royalty and other dignitaries. A member of one of the few black families in town, he spent many hours with Barney Spencer, the son of Al Spencer, exploring the woods around town. His father, who said his forefathers were Zulus, went to England as a young man of eighteen and was employed by a wealthy Scots family as a domestic servant. When he was twenty-six, Spencer along with Taylor's grandfather came to America with that family. When the Scots lost their money, they sold everything they had, including the Gordons. After the Civil War, Taylor's father and grandfather were in Ohio, where the younger man went to a school of domestic sciences and was trained as a chef. In Cairo, Illinois, where Taylor's grandfather died, his father met his future wife, Annie Goodlow.

The Gordons moved to Fort Benton, where the father worked as chef for a large gold-mining company until the company moved its headquarters back to Chicago. The Gordons stayed. The family liked the wide open spaces, decided to stay in Montana, and ended up in White Sulphur Springs, where Gordon senior worked as a chef at the

Higgins House. Gordon went to work on the Canadian Railway, hoping to make more money for his family, but was killed in a railroad accident in 1893, just two months before Taylor was born. Annie stayed in White Sulphur Springs and raised her family. There were six children: five boys and one girl. Arthur died of whooping cough at age one, but the rest of the family thrived.

Taylor Gordon in the 1920s

Taylor had a Huck Finn type of boyhood. He fished and hunted and, for cash, he collected bottles, delivered water, set bowling pins and did other odd jobs. One of his jobs was as messenger boy for the "ladies of the night" until his mother decided he was getting too old to work around the girls.

In his 1929 memoir *Born To Be,* Gordon drew a vivid picture of what it was like to grow up as a black man in White Sulphur Springs at the turn of the 20th century. His first jobs were working as a driver and he describes a few of his experiences. (All Gordon quotations are from this book.[4])

Unlike most medical resorts, the Springs are situated in the midst of a beautiful valley, and the roads around about are the finest for driving to be found anywhere. From three to five miles away rises in picturesque grandeur one of the most romantic ranges in all the Rocky mountains—a range whose recesses, defiles, summits, peaks and caverns, the homes of bears and lions, are yet unexplored. In fact, all the mountains that surround the valley are beautifully picturesque and very interesting to the explorer and abound in game. The streams that cross the valley abound in trout, and from them tons of finny beauties are taken every year. It is to the abundance of fish and game around this valley that the Indians owed their pleasure in this great medicine region, for while they were healing their maladies they could find plenty of game to subsist on without effort. There is probably no place on earth where nature has done more to combine the advantages of health and pleasure than this; and when it shall be refitted with the modern appliances of the age, which is to be done at an early date, it will stand without a rival as the health asylum and pleasure resort of the great Northwest....

After I learned to drive a car, I drove for pleasure for some time—maybe Barney's or Dick Manger's or John Potter's old Rambler. Then the Maytag company sent an agent into the valley with "the car of the century," a two lunged drive, two-seated bus. Their great selling point was that it could not get stuck on a hill. They had the gas tank above the engine. They stuck many a farmer on that bunch of junk. Cliff Tipton bought one and put it on the road for passengers between Dorsey and White

Sulphur Springs, twenty miles away. I drove it too. He
paid me sixty dollars a month.

I made a month or two with Tipton, and though he
was making money hand over fist, that wasn't enough
for him. He wanted me to drive day and night. One
morning I didn't get up at five o'clock to make an extra
run for him, so he took the car and burned the crank-
shaft bearing out, and I quit.

When he was hired, as a teenager, to drive for Ringling's
land company, the Smith River Development Company, it
was an eye-opener to this small-town boy. He wrote in his
memoir about this encounter with powerful easterners.

They had 90,000 acres of land, so it fell on me to drive
the guests out on the mountain trails in a big seven-pas-
senger air-cooled Franklin Six. They were amazed at
the beauty of the valley and surprised to know that I
didn't use a horn to warn people on the road. Warbling
was one of my best stunts. I also held honors for calling stock, when salting cattle. Not having any occasion
to make the stock call, I used this call for warning the
travelers on the road, as no native could or would let an
Easterner come in and get away without pulling his best
stunt.

The Ringling party only stayed ten days. During that
time there was one thing that happened that showed me
very plainly that Easterners were people of power and
conviction any time they had money. The Governor of
Montana had a business engagement with John Ringling
at eleven o'clock in the morning. Although awakened

many times, Ringling was not up yet, and didn't get up until one-thirty. The Governor was six men, he was so hot.… But he waited. I made up my mind then that the West was fine, but I wanted to be an Easterner.

Ringling was not intentionally rude—this was just how he lived his life. In his memoir, *The Circus Kings*, Henry Ringling North described his uncle's offbeat hours, noting that "he habitually breakfasted at three in the afternoon" and dinner was late in the evening.[5]

When L.N. Scott sent a ticket and money for Taylor to come to St. Paul, Minnesota, to be his chauffeur, Gordon set off on his quest to become an Easterner. This was where he first encountered discrimination far crueler than anything he had experienced in Montana. Instead of heading back to the safely of his Montana home, however, Taylor started work on the railway—working on trains that traveled from Chicago to Seattle, Portland and into Canada—but continuing east. As he neared New York, he sent a telegram to John Ringling, who was in New York, a telegram asking him for a job.

…New York bound. From St. Paul to Chicago my trip was like a short trolley ride, so many thoughts ran through my head. Everyone at home came before me in a vision. What would they say??? Emanuel Taylor Gordon—Mannie—Snowball—Old Zip—Blacky—in New York City—the biggest city in the U.S.A.! A feeling that comes once in a lifetime.

Awed by New York, Gordon went directly to John Ringling, sensing that the powerful man he had seen back in Montana would know how to tame this enormous city. Taylor's memoirs document Ringling's response.

His wonderful personality swept all fear I might have had into oblivion. I felt that no evil would happen to me soon. He put me in the hands of his butler, Ed, a colored man who had been with him for years. Ed gave me a room in the servants' quarters.

Taylor didn't see Ringling again until after his 1 P.M. breakfast. When the two encountered one another, Ringling had a proposition for him.

He asked me what I had been doing since I had left L.N. Scott. After I told him, he said, "Well, then, you can handle my private [railroad] car, can't you?" I told him I thought I could. "The car is in the B. & O. yards, Jersey City. Mrs. Ringling will give you a list for food. Get it filled at Summer Brothers' meat market on Sixth Avenue. I'll let you know when we are leaving town."

Thus Gorden was now heading to the South. "In two days' time," he recalled, "I was stocking up Ringling's private car, the *Wisconsin*, for a trip to Sarasota, Florida."

As Gordon traveled to the South, he was in for another lesson in racism. While it became clear to him that the Ringlings were powerful men, it also was very clear to him that the color of his skin defined his role in a more pronounced way in this part of the country. Writing in the slang of the day, he described it like this:

I soon found out that John Ringling and his brothers were big men in Sarasota. Everyone knew them as the rich Yankees, and anything or anybody connected with them became RINGLINGS. The day after my arrival, I was known as Ringling's Niggah. Niggah didn't mean anything, but to be a rich man's niggah—that established the amount of liberty the individual…was to have. The niggah of a man with a hundred thousand dollars couldn't do what a millionaire's niggah could do…Oh! no—not by a long shot.

At the Ringling estate in Sarasota Bay, the Ringling party played and rested in the southern sun. They fished almost daily. As Gordon noted, "Nearly every other day, their yachts could be seen leaving Sarasota Bay for the grouper banks, on a tarpon-fishing trip. I made some of those trips with them as chef."

After a trip to Chicago and back, John Ringling headed to Madison Square Garden in New York City. Gordon describes their return to New York on the train, then delves into an interesting peek into the domestic life of John Ringling.

Mr. Ringling returned for the great day, and I went with him. After two days work with the auto, carrying trunks and small things off of the private car brought from Florida, I locked it up and left it in the B. & O. private car yards in Jersey City. I didn't return to the car until the circus left New York for the road. I had a room in the servants' quarters on top of the high apartment house where Ringling lived. I didn't have much work to do at first in New York. Ed and Jessie were still with the

The Wisconsin *on exhibit in The Ringling, the circus museum in Sarasota.*

Ringlings. My duty was to keep Mr. Ringling's wardrobe in order, valet, all except shave him. He shaved himself. He said he never let a barber shave him—they ruined his face. He had a razor for each day in the week, the old-fashioned kind. He was a real Beau Brummell in those days, and particular! I remember one time he had four dozen shirts made by a Fifth Avenue shirt shop, and after wearing each one a coupla times, he didn't like the way they hung on his left shoulder, and had them all taken back. As a rule Mr. Ringling would be out of the house by two-thirty or three P. M., and I'd be right out after him. If I had to help do any cleaning in the morning, we were always through before either Mr. or Mrs.

Ringling were up, although Mrs. Ringling awoke early
nearly every morning.

So most every afternoon and evening, I would go
down to the [Madison Square] Garden or some other
theatre. I learned to tell every act in the circus by their
music and I got acquainted with most everyone around
the place.

Gordon did not generally travel with the circus, he traveled with John Ringling. One time, however, he described
a three-week period that the Ringlings spent with the circus before they took off on other business. He was in Mr.
Ringling's bedroom, putting the buttons in his shirt, when
Ringling told Gordon that they were going to travel as far as
Philadelphia with the circus. Taylor then described how the
traveling circus operated.

Everything worked like clockwork. Even the horses
that pulled up the tent-poles, knew when a post was in
the right position. They would stop by themselves—and
how they loved the crowds that watched them at work.
The men that put up and down the tents, they are the
proudest lot that ever lived. In all of Napoleon's career
never did he have a man under him that felt any more
honored and loyal than a tent hostler of the Big Top.

The ballet girls who worked in the circus were held to
their own moral code. During one season, there were a
hundred and fifty girls dancing in the King Solomon spectacle. The circus provided special cars for them, and they
had their own curfew at night. Every day, Sam McCracken

was preaching to them, according to Taylor Gordon, beginning with not to be seen "leaving hotels in the city in the daytime—it looks so crude." "Do leave the patrons alone on the circus grounds, for the business's respectability." When one girl got very unreasonable, John Ringling took charge of her and he threatened to pay her off. She told him, "God financed me at birth—don't worry about me" and bade him farewell with the "most unusual slang that made the long black cigar bounce from one side of Ringling's mouth to the other, his eyes blinking like a man who had been looking at the eclipse of the sun without smoked glasses."

TAYLOR GORDON DIDN'T TRAVEL WITH THE CIRCUS, HE TRAVELED WITH JOHN RINGLING

John Ringling never stayed with the show longer for more than three weeks, when Gordon was with him. "Many a trip was made to Oklahoma, where he built a railroad and developed an oil field," wrote Gordon.

In 1915, Ringling headed for Montana. As Taylor reported, "It was the Parberries."

In 1911, John Ringling had bought the Parberry House for $5500. It was Parberry who had bought Brewer Hot Springs in 1877, and platted White Sulphur Springs townsite. The house was one of two mansions on the west end of town, about two blocks from the station where the railcar was situated. After the Ringlings were settled in the house, Gordon became a yard man as well as chauffeur.

Gordon wanted to study voice, and several people in New York encouraged him to leave Ringling and take lessons. He went back and forth between Ringling and pursuing his singing career, finally going on tour as a concert

The Parberry-Ringling house's original appearance

tenor, accompanied by John Rosamond Johnson, and also as a member of Johnson's vaudeville act. Gordon's career peaked in 1927 when he toured France and England, performing for a number of dignitaries, including England's King George V and Queen Mary.

He continued to write and sing, and did some movie work the early 1930s. He never reclaimed his former level of success. He suffered a nervous breakdown and was hospitalized for some time. In 1959, he returned to White Sulphur Springs to live with his sister Rose Beatris Gordon. His later years were spent in some writing and concert performances. "Manny" sang at many weddings in the area. He died in 1971.

FROM TARPON-FISHING TO ART COLLECTING

By the 1920s, the Ringling Brothers and Barnum & Bailey Combined Shows were run by John and Charles. After Alf T. Ringling died on October 29, 1919, a "mist of jealousy rose to cloud their relationship" according to North in *The Circus Kings.* "If Uncle John got a yacht, the *Zalophus* (meaning sea lion), Uncle Charles had to have an even bigger one, the *Symphonia.* Because John had formed the Bank of Sarasota, Charles founded the Ringling Trust and Savings Bank."[6]

After they moved they also built rival multimillion-dollar homes in Florida by 1926 on land acquired during the 1920s Florida land boom. Charles and Edith Ringling's marble mansion was built on Sarasota Bay in 1925 and was decorated by Marshall Field and Company in Chicago. John and Mable Ringling's mansion, Ca' d'Zan (house of John), was built in 1925 and 1926. The largest home in Sarasota, it had thirty-one rooms, plus servant quarters.

On the many trips they made to Europe looking for circus acts, he and Mable collected art. They accumulated Old Master paintings that were displayed in their homes and in the auction houses of New York, and they purchased furnishing, tapestries, and paintings from New York's wealthy families. As with any of John's projects, this was done in a big way. On one occasion, he chartered a freighter to bring his purchases directly from Genoa to Port Tampa, Florida.[7]

After the Great Depression depleted John's finances, and Mable died, he married Emily H. Buck, but it was an unhappy relationship. As his health was declining, there was a great deal of dissension in the family business. John died of pneumonia on December 2, 1936, at the age of seventy in his Park Avenue home in New York.

His legacy lives on, however, in the John and Mable Ringling Museum of Art.

The museum, which John founded in 1926 to house his personal collection of masterpieces, features paintings and sculptures by the great Old Masters including the United States' greatest collection of Rubens, along with van Dyck, Velázquez, Titian, Tintoretto, Veronese, El Greco, Gainsborough and more. Because of delays in financing because of the Great Depression and the tangled family business, the museum was not finished until 1931, but it still continues to grow.[8]

Ca' d'Zhan when it was John and Mable's part-time home

SELLING THE MONTANA RANCH

The final chapter of John Ringling in Meagher County was the sale of the Ringling Isles Corporation to Wellington Rankin. John had retained vast properties in the county, and Rankin had leased it for many years. He and his associate, Arthur Aker, traveled to Florida to negotiate the sale from Ringling Isles.

The Jomar *private railcar was named by combining the first letters of John, Mable, and Ringling.*

Its original interior was ornately Victorian.

After John's death, nephew John Ringling North (seated) took over the circus, and the Jomar. *He redecorated its interior in contemporary style.*

The *Great Falls Tribune* of April 17, 1944, reported that

> Sale of the…ranch established by the late John Ringling…by the Ringling Isles Corp. to Wellington D. Rankin, Helena attorney, was announced today by George Weatherall, the corporation's Montana representative.…Ringling Isles, Inc. has managed the estate since 1934.
>
> One of the largest ranches in Montana, the property includes the Mayn and Heitman, or Birch creek ranch, the Catlin ranch and the Moss Agate ranch—63,000 acres of deeded property and 13–15,000 acres of leased property, Weatherall said.
>
> Rankin intends to run cattle on the ranch and operate it with the Dan Floweree Jr. and A.B. Cook ranches in Broadwater county and the Manuel Ranch in Meagher county, all of which he now owns and operates.

The sale ended John Ringling's presence in Montana.

1. Henry Ringling North and Alden Hatch. *The Circus Kings* (Garden City, NY: Doubleday & Company, 1960), 55-56.
2. Lee Rostad, *Mountains of Gold, Hills of Grass* (Martinsdale, MT: Bozeman Forks Publishing, 1994), 61-64.
3. Almon Spencer, diary, Meagher County Historical Society-White Sulphur Springs, Montana.
4. Taylor Gordon, *Born To Be*, New York: Covici-Friede Publishers, 1929 (reprint, Lincoln, NE: Bison Books, 1995).
5. North and Hatch, *The Circus Kings*, 56-58.
6. North and Hatch, *The Circus Kings*.
7. North and Hatch, *The Circus Kings*.
8. "Museum History," John and Mable Art Museum, http://www.ringling.org/ArtMuseum.aspx (accessed August 6, 2013).

The young Richard Ringling

CIRCUS PROMOTER, RANCHER, LAND SPECULATOR, RODEO ORGANIZER

RICHARD RINGLING (1895—1931)

THE SECOND RINGLING to make an appearance in Montana was Richard, the only son of Alfred T. Ringling, or "Alf T."

Richard was raised in the original permanent headquarters town of Baraboo, Wisconsin, where the original five Ringling brothers built comfortable homes to replace the old sleeping-dining car they had used in the early days of traveling with the circus. John North noted in his book *The Circus Kings* that the car had been "not really a luxury at all but a necessity, since they and their wives, especially Al [Albert] and Charles, spent a great part of their lives on the circus train."[1]

According to North, Richard Ringling was loved by the uncles and indulged by his father, perhaps more so after 1914, when Alf T. and Della went through an acrimonious divorce. Richard was eighteen and stayed with his father, but Della received custody of Marjorie, a baby the Ringlings had adopted in 1911.

North described his cousin Richard as a colorful character. "He was the best companion, the wittiest, the most imaginative, and the worst spoiled of all my cousins."

E.E. MacGilvra of Butte, always called "Boo" (for Baraboo), a colorful politician and lobbyist who served on the Montana Historical Society for more than twenty years and was a state senator from Lake County for many sessions, grew up with Richard Ringling. He described how this relationship developed, in an interview with editor Vivian Paladin of *Montana: The Magazine of Western History.*

> I grew up in the circus world of the Ringling Brothers, who got their start in Baraboo a couple of decades earlier. I say I grew up with the circus because Dick Ringling of Baraboo, Wisconsin, was my best friend. With my aunt as tutor, Dick and I traveled with the circus for eight seasons, and we saw every part of the country, even including Montana a time or two.

MacGilvra described Richard's mother, Mrs. Alf. T. as "a hen with just one chick." She wanted Richard to travel with the circus and her husband, but Richard didn't want to. He would rather, as MacGilvra noted, stay "home and ride his pony with me and shoot marbles and go to the swimming hole." Mrs. Ringling's solution was to invite Boo MacGilvra along, so he grew up alongside Richard, with the aunt/tutor, traveling with the circus. It was, recalled MacGilvra, a marvelous education.

RICHARD PREFERRED BOYHOOD ADVENTURES IN BARABOO TO TRAVELING WITH THE CIRCUS

Besides learning all about the circus, getting to know the people (yes, the strange ones, too) and the animals and the marvelous logistics of this grand show, I also acquired my great love for history. This aunt of mine was a history buff, and every town we'd go to she knew something about its past. Mr. Ringling would furnish us with a team of Arabian ponies, a buggy and a good driver and we'd explore and we'd learn and we'd be quizzed about it later.

Sounds like we were ideal little Lord Fauntleroy's, doesn't it, learning our lessons and toeing the mark? But Dick and I did something once that I don't know yet I should talk about. But it turned out all right, so I'll tell you.

Mr. Ringling had paid quite a price for a beautiful little filly that became his pride and joy and his pet saddle mare. She was a beauty! One terribly hot day in August, when everyone had gone into the big top, even all the trainers and hostlers with the animals, Dick and I realized that Mr. Ringling's filly had developed a sudden urge to partake of the forbidden fruit. The only animal left in the area was an energetic old zebra jack and he was soon whiffin' the air. We decided maybe this was the time to make dreams come true.

"I'll go get the filly," Dick said, "and you grab the jack." Dick backed the beautiful little lady up to a small manure pile, and I got hold of the jack. He knew where he was headed—he came near pulling me off my feet. Well, of course, things happened faster'n hell can scorch a feather.

We didn't peep about what we had done, and no one had witnessed the deed. In due time, along about fall, this filly starts filling out. Mr. Ringling gives the boss hostler the dickens for overfeeding her and the hostler swore to God he hadn't. Along in the spring, she shells out this zebroid colt—half zebra and half American saddler. Mr. Ringling is heartbroken, ready to kill anybody who had pulled such a shabby stunt.

But as this colt grew older, it became a beauty. It was kind of a red chestnut and it had faint stripes around its hocks, kind of over its rump and withers—a few stripes on its face down to around its chest. You could stand it in the sun and you could see faint stripes shining through on its sides.

Alf T.'s mansion overlooked the R.T. Richard Circus winter quarters

Well, you know, Mr. Ringling got so he loved that colt and he broke him out for a pet saddle horse. After nearly 80 years, I still don't know whether I should claim any credit for helping hatch this handsome critter or be ashamed of it.[2]

RICHARD RINGLING'S EARLY BUSINESS VENTURES

Early on, the colorful Richard decided to try his hand at running a billiard parlor on New York's Broadway, which attracted a variety of entertainers, theater people, and gamblers, according to writer David Lewis Hammarstrom in *Big Top Boss*.

Then, in 1917, Richard wanted to take out his own show, so Alf T. set him up a with a "truck" circus that was small but completely equipped. In order to distinguish this circus from the main Ringling business, it was named the R.T. Richard Circus. In the March 1942 issue of *Bandwagon*, one of his managers recalled his time with the circus. F.M. Farrell recalled that season of 1917 as one of the most memorable in his twenty-year career with circuses. After placing an ad in *Billboard* for work, Farrell received the following reply.

R.T. Richards Supreme Show of the World, Great European Circus of superb Novelties, Mighty Menagerie of Rare Wild Animals, Stupendous Spectacular Pageant; Immense New Museum of Strange Marvels, Gorgeous Free Street Parade, and Mammoth Imposing Horse Fair. New York offices—West 42th Street. The absolute perfection of all tented displays.

After Farrell signed a contract to work the show, doing

"side show magic, Punch & Judy, ventriloquist act" as well as "lecturing," he realized that R.T. Richard was Richard T. Ringling, the name reversed so as not to conflict with the Ringling Brothers Circus. The R.T. Richard Circus began and ended at the home of Richard's father, Alf T. , who had a vast estate at Oak Ridge, New Jersey. Although Farrell never saw it himself, he described it as including "a beautiful stone mansion, an artificial lake, stone gate houses and arched horse shoe gates built of massive stone."

In the February 9, 1919, *Billboard*, Farrell had described the show itself as a walking spectacle, with cages of animals and elephants that walked from town to town.

The show traveled by wagon and had a few trucks at the opening of the season. The bandwagon was a truck with a tableau body having paintings on each side. A truck bandwagon was a novelty at that time. All cages and tableaus were wagons drawn by horses, and the parade was better and longer than that of a 15 car RR show. More horses were carried than a 15 car show would be able to transport.

The five elephants walked from town to town and walking on pavement and stepping on stones, sometimes their feet would get sore, so they used to put leather boots on their feet. On the morning of June 20th going from Lee, Mass., to Chester, they went through the Berkshire Hills. For several miles there was a dense woods on each side of the road. A motorist coming up behind the elephants blew his horn, which scared them and they stampeded into the woods. They rounded up four of them that afternoon and got the fifth one late

R.T. Richard, aka Richard Ringling, at right.

next day. They got into Huntington the night of the 21st of June just after the night performance. So the show didn't have the advertised herd of elephants in Chester or Huntington. The July 4th stand was Fitchburg, Mass., where we celebrated by having three special meals.

The show went on through New England, New York City, then on to New Jersey and Maryland, performers and animals setting up, performing one or two shows a day, then breaking down and traveling on. It was a grueling schedule.

The show after touring New England for the summer, returned to New York State at Rye, Aug. 26, and most of the performers spent the afternoon and evening at Rye Beach. Showed in Rye Monday Aug. 27th, Mamaroneck 28th, and North Phelan 29th. Then into New York City,

Aug. 30 to Sept 1st showing on 143 St., off Lennon Avenue. Labor Day stand was Union Hill, N.J., the show spent 13 days in New Jersey, the last stand being Lambertville Sept. 14th, Doylestown, Pa., Sept. 15 and several stands in Penna., then into Delaware and Eastern Maryland.

The Sept. 26th stand was Newark, Del. The show was in early and set up in time for an afternoon performance, but the stringer truck got lost. As they couldn't put seats up without stringers we had to blow the afternoon show. So came evening and still no stringers and time to open the doors to the Big Show. We opened the side show on time and packed them in. The Management announced shortly after eight that there would be no night show on account of "no seats." The crowd yelled "We will stand up" so the show went on with the audience standing. Farrell went on, in the *Billboard* interview:

In some cities, the circus did not receive as warm a welcome. When the circus arrived in Delaware City, Delaware on October 3, the posters advertising the circus were covered with theater bill posters. When the advance crew arrived in town, they were asked why this was allowed to happen, as the show would close the season on that Saturday. We had a good day's business even if our paper had been covered.

Richard traveled with the circus until the middle of the season when financial woes brought an early retreat to winter quarters. The next year, Alf T. took the circus out. When the circus closed on October 6, 1917, in Media, Pennsylvania, Farrell said they celebrated with a farewell chicken dinner. As the crew and performers were eating, Alf T. Ringling stood up before the crowd and told them that if the war was over that winter, the show would go out again in the spring. If the war did not end, the show would not go out. In the spring of 1918, Alf T. was too ill to take the show out.

The circus performers, animals and crew moved on to Alf T.,'s country estate in Oak Ridge, New Jersey. Until they could be disposed of the lions and tigers were housed in the big stables, where their ululations shattered the peace of the well-groomed New Jersey countryside. Animals were housed in formal brick stables with their coach house and box stalls, courtyard and belvedere with a gilt trotting horse weather vane.

By 1918, only thirteen railroad circuses were on tour, two of which were owned by the Ringlings. Henry died of heart disease on October 10, 1918, in Baraboo, Wisconsin, leaving his brothers Alf T., Charles and John the remaining three partners, running the circus. In fall 1918, Charles and John Ringling merged the Ringling Brothers Circus and the Barnum & Bailey show and moved the show to winter headquarters in Bridgeport, Connecticut, which was a considerable emotional and economic shock to the residents of Baraboo. Bridgeport had been the winter headquarters for the Barnum & Bailey show even after the Ringlings bought it in 1907, but this was the first time the Ringling show had not returned to Baraboo since 1884.

WESTWARD HO!

From the trunk circus, Richard next headed to White Sulphur Springs, Montana, where his flamboyant uncle, John Ringling, had purchased land as early as 1903. Richard was to help with his uncle's land business, but soon was busy building his own land base.

When Richard arrived in White Sulphur Springs in 1917, he encountered an up-and-coming small town. When F. Scott Fitzgerald had visited the area in 1915, according to Landon Jones, in *Montana: The Magazine of Western History*, he found the town was a lively and interesting place, "a weather-beaten mining, ranching and farming community with 500 citizens and a thriving saloon and red light district. Some mines had fizzled, but the wettest spring in years was producing bumper crops of grains, hay and alfalfa."[3]

Richard soon met the attractive daughters of Powell Black, Aubrey and Olga Black, who were considered the belles of the town. Powell and Mary Etta Alice Black had come to Montana in 1892 when they were headed for the state of Washington, but Powell's uncle, Preston Lesley, who was Montana's territorial governor, recommended instead that they settle in White Sulphur Springs.

Along with the Black girls, Richard quickly joined the group of young people, including John Potter who became a good friend and a business partner. The son and namesake of an early settler, prominent sheep rancher and banker, John Potter, Jr., graduated from the Montana Agricultural College in Bozeman as an electrical engineer. He served in the army as a first lieutenant from 1917 until 1920. When he returned to White Sulphur Springs, he worked for Richard Ringling, working with the circus as well as promoting rodeos around the country. He eventually became vice president of the Bozeman Roundup until he left with Ringling in 1926. With Ringling's help, Potter later opened and operated an abstract and insurance business and served for a time as both a representative and then a senator in the State Legislature.

RICHARD'S WEAK HEART MADE THE ARMY REJECT HIM FOR WWI
Ringling registered for the draft in White Sulphur Springs and entered as a health condition a weak heart.

On January 11, 1918, Richard married Aubrey Black. As the White Sulphur Springs *Meagher Republican* reported to a town hungry for every detail:

> ...the home wedding took place at 1 o'clock this afternoon when Richard T. Ringling and Miss Aubrey Barlow Black were united in marriage by the Rev. George Barber at the home of the bride. The bridesmaid was Miss Francis Peacock, and Lieutenant J.V. Potter acted as groomsman.… A profusion of beautiful and expensive wedding gifts were admired by the guests. The groom's gift to the bride, a handsomely designed platinum bracelet, studded with diamonds was among them. …
>
> The bride and groom left immediately after the ceremony going to Ringling by motor, where they took the train for Chicago. Later they will go to Tampa, Florida, where they will spend the remainder of the winter. They will be accompanied as far as Chicago by Lieutenant Potter, who is going east to enter service in the ordinance department of the United States Army.
>
> The bride was born in White Sulphur Springs and

is the daughter of Mr. and Mrs. Powell Black, recently deceased. With the exception of a few months spent visiting at the former home of her mother in Tennessee she has spent practically her whole life here and her natural charm and grace of manner have won for her a large number of warm friends, and most loyal of whom being the ones who know her best. She met Mr. Ringling last summer, and their mutual admiration soon ripened into love, today's ceremony being the culmination of a pretty romance.

The groom's home is in Baraboo, Wis, although his extensive farming interests here require his attention at different seasons of the year. He is the son of G.H. [actually A.T.] Ringling, one of the Ringling Brothers, of circus fame and is heir to a large estate. Mr. Ringling has purchased several tractors and will farm a large acreage here next spring and summer.

Luxurious apartments and a yacht await the happy couple at Tampa, Florida, and the honeymoon will be spent amid ideal surroundings They will return to White Sulphur Springs…in April.

The two did spend part of their honeymoon on John's yacht in Florida. John and Mable Ringling had no children and were very fond of Richard and embraced Aubrey as well. They had many visits back and forth over the years and had a very close relationship.

Richard was handsome, musical, had a good sense of humor and was eager to embrace new and different things. Leading a privileged life, he had plenty of money and perhaps not as much good judgment about protecting his interests. He was ready to become a rancher in Montana. Aubrey was a beautiful, well educated woman—part of the upper social class in a small town, but she accepted her role in the family of wealth and prestige with equanimity. Over the years of their marriage, Richard often relied on her help and judgment.

As Theresa Buckingham said in a *Montana CattleWomen* column, Aubrey, who she described as "small, elegant, practical and direct," was also a good manager, "with the talents of one 'to the manor born'." Her domain was large. There were imbroglios but she controlled them."[4]

They bought the Parberry House, which John and Mable Ringling had bought in 1911, and now sold to Richard for $1. After adding a large two-story addition on the south side, the house had twenty-six rooms with suites for Richard, Aubrey, the children, and guests. Richard remodeled the basement to house a bar and a liquor safe. Richard and Aubrey entertained often and well. They had three children, Jane, Mable, and Paul. Young Paul, the eldest of the three, remembers helping roll whiskey barrels down the incline to the basement.

The second year of their marriage, Aubrey went on the road with the circus during the summer. She told the *Meagher County News* in 1935:

> I traveled right along, eating in the cook tent and getting acquainted with everybody. You can imagine that was a thrilling experience for a girl who had never been anywhere or seen anything—outside the Rocky Mountains.[5]

● ● ●

Theresa Buckingham in a later *CattleWomen* column described the Ringlings' effect on the residents of the small town of White Sulphur Springs. Although the Ringling circus "with the prancing horses with tossing plumes and spangles" never arrived, Ringling's residence in town was "indeed a spectacular time for a little western town."

The surprising and innovative programs launched by Richard Ringling kept the valley in a state of wonder, with their log houses and pole corrals, skeptical of what was to come of all this. The townspeople stood back—but only briefly. No one had to peek over the back fence at the garden party where Richard Ringling was. He was inclusive with his invitations. Easy-going and fun-loving, he had a talent for mixing his eastern friends with his western neighbors, and everyone had fun. His advisors, his help and his drinking companions came from the local people as much as from the show business and dude ranch circles....

WHITE SULPHUR SPRINGS RESIDENTS OFTEN WENT TO SARASOTA AS TEMPORARY STAFF IN THE WINTERS

With the family's easy relationship with the community, the staff was often stretched to include the townspeople. It was not unusual, for example, to hear, "Aunt Carrie Zehntner is going to Florida with the Ringling's. She is to help with the children on the train."

Ringlings are taking Bill Hensley to Sarasota for the winter. They have some work there they want him to do.

The local last worked for them on a full time basis with the stock and also at large dog kennels. Just about everyone at some time or other worked at the ranches.

Most high school boys could brag that they had played pool in the basement recreation room, even though none of the children in the family were then at that age. It was a common sight along a country road to meet the children in their pony cart loaded with small friends they had picked up along the way. Aubrey, trim and suntanned in ranch clothes, silver Indian jewelry and custom made boots, always took time for an unhurried chat with old friends or ranch hands sunning themselves on the "sheepherders' side" of Main Street. She never forgot a name or a face or a ranch....Her charities were prompted because she knew when people were in need...

The house, now on a truly grand scale, was furnished with massive mahogany, teakwood, tapestries and Tiffany lamps. A large Tiffany lamp hanging over the dining room had a bullet hole in it. There were as many tales about how the bullet hole got there as there are colors in Tiffany glass.

The cellar, they say, was stocked on schedule, by bootleggers arriving in three big open touring cars...The liquor bottles were not in cases, but individually wrapped in burlap and tied in sacks...

Big flashy cars moved regularly along the dusty Main Street. Everyone looked important and probably everyone was. They say the poker games were legendary. "They say,"—"They say." Everyone had a story embellished according to the creativity of the teller.[6]

Aubrey's sister Olga was married in 1915 to John Kirkup in Butte. Kirkup worked for a lumber company in Anaconda. The marriage was a short one, and a year after Richard and Aubrey married, she married Lester Work of Gallatin County, a wool buyer and sheep man. This marriage ended in divorce in 1919, however, the brothers-in-law, Ringling and Work, went into the ranching business together, buying the Clear Range Ranch from John Ringling in 1921 and operating as Ringling and Work. Work was in charge of the sheep. The Ringlings chose Work as Paul's godfather in 1920.

The *Meagher Republican* of September 26, 1919, reported:

The Birch Creek ranch, one of the finest ranch properties in the state of Montana, was sold Wednesday by John Ringling to Story &Work giving the later concern one of the biggest properties in the west, and one that will run close to 40,000 sheep. With the ranch, the purchasers took the stock and part of the horses. The property was then consigned to Richard Ringling and Lester Work.

The property consists of 29,000 acres, and purchaser assumed about $100,000 dollars worth of the Ringling livestock in the deal, making the total figure a little short of half a million dollars.

The ranch is an ideal stack property, well improved, and cuts a fine crop of hay.

In 1923, ownership changed and the papers reported that a big deal had just been concluded with the signing of papers by virtue of which Richard T. Ringling takes over the entire Ringling and Work interests in the Smith River Valley. All stock and ranches were included in the transaction and in future the business will be conducted by Mr. Ringling alone. Work continued for Richard as his sheep foreman. More than 110,000 acres of land are involved. Mr. Ringling's holdings are increased to an enormous acreage which extends the entire length of the valley, beginning with the old Hayman ranch on Sixteen. Further down on the south fork of the Smith River is the Moss Agate ranch. On Birch Creek, he now owns the onetime Mayn and Heitman ranches and further down the valley has acquired the Len Lewis ranch, later called the Clear Range, and still further down the valley on the Smith River the ranch which was once the property of John Moore. On the outskirts of White Sulphur Springs are the Dairy farm and the Mark Hunt place.

By 1925, Richard had over 95,000 acres that included the Birch Creek Ranch, Catlin Lake Ranch, Catlin Ranch, Enfield Ranch, Crosby Ranch, Moss Agate Ranch, Roscoe Ranch and the Hayman Ranch and some lots in town.

LAND OF MILK AND HEREFORDS

In 1916, John Ringling had established a dairy herd, the seed stock of the cattle herd from the famous stock of John Kelly of Wisconsin. In 1920 and 1921, additional stock was purchased from the Helena Holstein and Anaconda Willow Glen herds. Ringling had planned at one time to develop stock for the European market, devastated by the war.

Richard had his own stock, and in the early 20s took his cows to shows, winning more than 150 trophies in a few short years. Managed by J. G. Coleman, the herd boasted winners such as Rose Glen DeKol Arline, a Montana champion butterfat producer, and Alcartra Johann DeKol Burke the 6th, a champion who kept up her record milk produc-

*Richard Ringling's
massive dairy barn*

tion, despite the fact that she was exhibited from county fair to country fair.

The herd was housed in a 360 feet by 40 feet barn, with a 100 feet extension. The main building had 100 stanchions for testing and calving. The building was considered a marvel of engineering in the area, as it contained automatic drinking troughs that supplied water at an even temperature, a luxury far beyond the means of most Montana dairy ranchers. Conveyors on overhead tracks distributed hay, silage, bedding, and collected milk, which reduced hand labor to a minimum. Bedding straw was blown from the stacker into the windmow. The main mow had a capacity of 400 tons, which was filled from Ringling's 1,000 acres of alfalfa. The Ringlings also raised grain, sunflowers, and corn to help make up the 400 tons of silage they used each year.

More than 300 gallons of milk were delivered to the creamery daily, and 100 ranchers were on the payroll weekly for bringing in cream. Only sweet cream was accepted, and the creamery demanded the cleanest of standards. As the dairy herd increased, so did the production

of cream, and in 1925, the creamery installed its own cold storage plant with a capacity of 15,000 pounds, iced from an ammonia refrigeration plant. In its first year of operation, the creamery made 75,000 pounds of butter. By 1924, the 130,000 pounds of butter produced supplied customers on the transcontinental Milwaukee Railway, as well as the Milwaukee Railway's Gallatin Gateway Hotel, Butte's Finlan Hotel and Helena's Eddy's Cafe.

Ranches and farmers benefited from the herd by being able to buy calves or bulls from the purebred stock. In addition Ringling built a number of dairy barns on ranches around the county—on either Ringling owned ranches or those in which he partnered with the owner. These barns were built of the best materials with hardwood floors. Today, the only one of these barns is on the Birch Creek Ranch.

Because no expense was spared, the Ringling dairy herd and creamery were the finest of its kind, although the Ringling Dairy had trouble competing among the other dairies in Montana that operated on less overhead.

Mr. Ringling will maintain four melding herds of

Detail from a huge panoramic view of competitors, performers, and Shriners involved in the 1926 Bozeman Roundup. The event was one of Richard Ringling's favorite projects. His family and visiting friends watch the action from the private seating near the center of this image. COURTESY OF LAURA POTTER McMILLAN

Holsteins under his own management, these being at
the Ringling dairy farm, where he has just completed
the finest barn in the state and which is probably one of
the largest dairy barns in the West, the Hunt place, The
R.T.R. ranch at Dorsey and the Birch creek ranch.

In 1922, F.A. McDonald and R.T. Ring-
ling purchased the Kinyon Ranch at Mule **RICHARD BEGAN**
Creek, Ft. Logan, consisting of 1320 acres **CONSOLIDATING AREA**
and the Shade Place at Hussey Creek of **RANCHES INTO A HUGE**
420 acres.
DAIRY FARM
The plan was to turn the ranches into
dairy farms and the Kinyon Place to run over seventy-five
dairy cows, and the Shade Place about fifty. They expected
to be able to make the ranches both good producers.

The lake site, covering about 300 acres, had been used as
a reservoir for the Shade place. Plans were for the enlarge-
ment of the irrigation project to irrigate 1500 acres.

Ringling then bought the Mark Hunt property, east of
town, of 240 acres. The Hunt Ranch was considered an ideal
dairy ranch. Hussey had a herd of Purebred Holsteins that
he sold to the Hollywood farms in California. The few that
he retained he sold to Ringling. The barn was said to have
modern dairy equipment. Ringling immediately put a crew
to repaint the buildings.

In the summer of 1922, the *Meagher Republican* reported:

In order to assure the handling of 500 head of dairy
cows, to supply the products for the new creamery
which he is building. R.T. Ringling has evolved a new
plan of building up dairy farms, stocking them and rent-

ing them to practical farmers on a fifty-fifty basis. The idea has already been put into operation in a dozen places, and it is more than likely that before Mr. Ringling's plans are entirely carried thru, 50,000 acres of his land will be utilized for the production of milk products.

Without a question the idea is feasible, and will go a long way toward mending the fortunes of town and valley and to hasten the return of better times locally."

…The plan would ultimately result in making profitable dairy farms of a large number of isolated farms…

…Operator must have the needed equipment with which to till the soil and haying machinery sufficient to handle that end. He must have horses, but cattle and hogs will be furnished, and the rent will have a half the increase. Wherever possible, Mr. Ringling encourages… raising…additional beef stock, and grain for market in order to give the farms added income. The opportunities to start dairy farming in the Smith River valley are thus made comparatively easy and thus opportunity of success multiplied.

The owner will furnish lumber and carpenters for construction of the new buildings, will pay half threshing bills, furnish breeding stock as well as furnish all material for fences. About the greatest expense the operator has is for seed grain. The proceeds are divided fifty-fifty.

Among the farms that have been turned to dairy purposes recently are the following:

Section 5, near Ringling, leased to Mr. Eldridge, who has a herd of 25 Holsteins.

Moss Agate unit, of two sections to Mr. Ringer, who is

now milking 30 cows and who will this fall milk 50 head of Holsteins.

1320 acre Kinyon property, near Fort Logan, which was leased to a firm, Francis, Crosby and Francis, who have 20 cows now and will have 609 head next year...

Shade ranch of about one section now being investigated by Billings parties which will run as 25 head of Holsteins.

The Crosby Ranch of two sections, where Hire & son will run a herd of 50 Holsteins.

Woods Gulch property of one section which will probably be taken over by John Walsh of Billings.

Newlan Creek section, a particularly fine hay section, which property has just been taken over by outside people and which will run 25 Holsteins.

The list comprises only a few of the places which were ready for occupancy. Most of the places will require fence changes, new buildings, and considerable improvements before they will be already to maintain dairy herds properly.

Mr. Ringling will maintain four melding herds of Holsteins under his own management, these being at the Ringling dairy farm, where he has just completed the finest barn in the state and which is probably one of the largest dairy barns in the West, the Hunt place, The R.T.R. ranch at Dorsey and the Birch creek ranch.

The dairy barns Ringling built were of the best materials and survived many years. One remains today at the Birch Creek Ranch.

Ringling also bought the Robert Kaufman property that

included a meat market, buildings and the slaughter house property. Ringling bought the business to supply the Ringling ranches in the valley, but assured people that the fully equipped market would also be open to the public.

DAIRY CATTLE AND A PEA-CROP CANNERY

The station was moved closer to the track and a creamery built on that site. Work on the creamery in town continued through the fall of 1922. Half of the 40x80 building was for the dairy and half to be used for a feed and produce store, the creamery intending to deal in feeds for dairy purposes, poultry and poultry products. Upstairs to be living quarters for the employees.

A carload of pure-bred Jerseys and Guernseys from Baraboo came into Ringling one evening after eight days on the road. Mr. Miller was in charge of the herd. He put them in the stockyards at Ringling and came back in the morning to find about half of them gone. He loaded the ones there and sent them by special train to the Hunt Place at White Sulphur Springs. Dr. C.H. Wight and Clarence Chambers loaded their saddle horses in the car and went to Ringling and after a few inquiries started in search of the wandering cattle, which they located about eight miles north of Ringling. A calf born on the train was taken to the livery station at Ringling, and then transferred to the train for White Sulphur Springs, riding in the engine.

The creamery opened on January 23, 1923. Two years later, the *Havre Daily Promoter* reported:

The Springs Civic Club is arranging to have a Buffet luncheon commencing at 10 A.M. This will be at the

I.O.O.F. hall and all are invited to come and get some of the famous Dreidlin "hot dog" and a good cup of coffee. There will be interesting talks by members of the College at Bozeman and an inspection trip through the Creamery and also the big Ringling barn.

The Springs Creamery company, organized two years ago has proven itself to be a potent factor in the prosperity of the valley. During 1924 the creamery produced 130,766 pounds of butter, which was sold for $49,691.08, and fully one-half of the butter fat was furnished by the small farmers of the valley, according to H.J. Long, manager...In addition, the creamery made and sold approximately $3,000 worth of ice cream, which gives the creamery a business of nearly $54,000 for the year 1924.

Improvements made during 1924 were chronicled in the *Meagher Republican* on September 15 of that year:

The creamery installed a refrigerating and ice plant, that will accommodate 5,000 pounds of butter. Because the demand for butter exceeds the supply at the present time, there was no immediate need for the additional storage room. However, the concern looks toward increased output in the near future. A power line has been strung in the creamery plant, doing away with the necessity of steam power....Richard Ringling is the owner of one of the largest and best equipped dairy plants west of the Mississippi, J.H. Healey is manager of the dairy. We are milking about 460 registered Holstein cows in our plant at WSS," said Mr. Ringling yesterday, "and make an average of 100,000 pounds of butter a month."

Mr. Ringling plans to have 50 head of show cattle in all the important fairs and shows in the east this fall. He expects to place sentries in Iowa, Illinois, Wisconsin, at the Minnesota state fair and end the season with prize winners of the International Hay and Grain Show at Chicago. The Springs Creamery company, organized two years ago has proven itself to be a potent factor in the prosperity of the valley. During 1924 the creamery produced 130,766 pounds of butter, which was sold for $49,691.08, and fully one-half of the butter fat was furnished by the small farmers of the valley, according to H.J. Long, manager of the company. In addition, the creamery made and sold approximately $3,000 worth of ice cream, which gives the creamery a business of nearly $54,000 for the year 1924.

THE CREAMERY COULD STORE 5,000 POUNDS OF BUTTER

The herd was sold after Ringling's death in October of 1931. In those days of Depression the bidding was mild, although there were many observers. There was still interest in the Ringling herd although "Rather timid bidding characterized the first day of bidding."

Eyeing the get of the Pacific International champion Holstein bull of 1928 and 1929, prospective bids were here from many parts of Montana and from Idaho, Washington and Wisconsin.

The newspapers, in March of 1925, announced that Richard Ringling was joining forces with Col. William L. White, who "has been placing settlers on western lands for the past five years and farms a 1,000 acre ranch on his own account."

Ringling and White planned to "colonize" 100,000 acres of land in the Smith River valley. The land was to provide the peas for a pea cannery in White Sulphur Springs, according to the *Meagher County News*.

The colonizing undertaking is being handled from New York by Ringling-White, Inc. and is of the most ambitious character. The pea land is being cut up into small farms of from 40 to 80 acres, and the land is sold to settlers on long time payments, with nothing due, except taxes for two years. Buildings, as required by the purchasing farmer, or building material sold to him at wholesale prices. Livestock and farm equipment will also be furnished at the lowest possible prices.

Through the dairy and pea canning plant a good market will be afforded for everything the settler will produce and he will have the advice of an experienced agriculturist, familiar with local soil conditions, to guide him to success.

The cannery never materialized despite continuing interest.

The large cattle barn burned in 1932. Holding hands, Paul and his sister Jane stood and watched the large structure afire. The silos stood on the town's horizon for many years before being torn down.

THE BOZEMAN ROUNDUP

Richard's most beloved project, he stated, was the Bozeman Roundup, which began after World War I.

During the summer of 1919, construction began on what was to become a centerpiece of Gallatin Valley entertainment for twelve all too short years. Thomas Byron Story and his brother Nelson, Jr. got together with R.P. McClelland and Lester Work to build a stadium and grandstand on a four-block tract just south of the present county fairgrounds. The site cost three thousand dollars and the construction expenditure rose to twenty-eight thousand dollars. The grandstand would seat 2,800 people; the stadium would accommodate 15,000 to 20,000 customers. The builders had to act fast, the Elks would be in town for their yearly convention in mid August—a good time to make money. On July 14, the Kenyon Noble lumber yard brought in the first load of wood for construction. The Story brothers hired returning veterans to do the work, but they were non-union and had to cross picket lines. Despite the labor troubles, the stadium and quarter mile racetrack were finished twenty-eight days later, ready for the first Roundup celebration.

August 12 began with a morning parade down Main Street, featuring rodeo cowboys and cowgirls, Flathead Indians in full regalia, Roundup queen Peg McGovern, and other local and state dignitaries. After the parade, the crowds enjoyed a baseball game and an Elks carnival. The actual Roundup rodeo competition took place in the middle of the afternoon, with cowboys and cowgirls competing for purses of several hundred dollars each in bronc and bull riding, horse racing, trick riding, and bulldogging. In the

Charles M. Russell painted the steerhead logo for the Bozeman Roundup. COURTESY OF LAURA POTTER MCMILLAN

evening, local residents and visiting Elk members watched a minstrel show, the latest Gene Quaw musical revue called *Hello, Bill,* and danced in the middle of Main Street and Central Avenue.

For the next six years, Bozeman had a good position on the rodeo circuit; cowboy stars regularly performed here as they did in Madison Square Garden in New York; Calgary, Alberta; Pendleton, Oregon; and as far south as Mexico. A small number of female performers charmed crowds along the way. Dressed in costumes of their own design, trimmed with bits of fur, sequins, and bright sashes, topped with giant brimmed hats, these women dared to compete in bronc riding, bull riding, and bulldogging, events not open to women today. Each afternoon, after the rodeo clowns, the crowds warmed up the festivities, shouting the slogan, "She's wild! She's wild! She's wild!"[5]

The stadium was surrounded by decorated Indian tepees. Not too far away, crowds thronged around something called the "Slippery Gulch," a gambling operation which included two roulette wheels, a chuck-a-luck wheel, two faro tables, and one for blackjack. Threading through the people, rodeo officials (distinguished by their white silk shirts featuring brightly colored butterflies embroidered on the sleeves and a bucking bronco on the back), saw to it that their customers had a good time without breaking too many laws. Bogart's Grove, a park and auto camp south of East Main Street near Church Avenue, filled with tents...[6]

In 1921, the four owners of the Bozeman Roundup approached Richard Ringling to finance the building of the new stadium. Instead, he bought the organization and then built the new stadium. Richard T. Ringling continued the yearly events until August 5 and 6, 1926. Shortly thereafter, lightning struck the grandstand, badly scarring the wooden structure. The building was condemned and torn down for salvage lumber in 1932.

The National Association, established by Ringling, furnished stock and produced rodeos across the country including Ellensburg, Washington; New York; Bozeman; and Tucson, Arizona—scheduled by John Potter, Ringling's associate. One of Paul Ringling's early memories was being in Oregon with John Mullens, a key member of the rodeo family.

Potter of White Sulphur Springs was in charge of advertising in 1922 and later became the vice president of the Bozeman Association. Potter's father was an early stockman in the area. He helped found and served as president for the Bank of Meagher County (First National Bank) resigning to take a partnership role in buying the Clendennin Ranch at Martinsdale. He managed the ranch for ten years until his retirement.

John Potter was graduated from the State Agricultural college at Bozeman as an electrical engineer. At the beginning of the World war, he took training at the Westinghouse company's plant in Springfield, Mass., and was commissioned a first lieutenant in the ordnance department. Later he was stationed at Detroit and then at Washington with jurisdiction over four states. When mustered out in 1920, he returned to White Sulphur Springs, and for the next six years, worked for Richard Ringling in promoting rodeos around the country. He was vice president of the Bozeman Stampede that Ringling bought in 1922.

It was Potter who contacted C.M. Russell to paint a logo for the stampede. Russell did a small water color of a steer head from which the logo was developed. (This art is now on loan by Laura Potter McMillan to the Montana Historical Society, Helena.) Russell was also invited to the stampede, but illness prevented his attending.[7]

In 1922, under Ringling, the Roundup was held for four days in August. It was a $50,000 production, offering $12,000 in cash prizes. It advertised an arena seating 20,000 people with 2,000 seats in the grandstand. On opening day, 10,000 people attended.

The Bozeman show continued each year. Hundreds of

private homes were opened to visitors, and a camp ground had 500 campers. They arranged with the college for housing if needed in buildings still under construction. Ringling also furnished the bucking horses for the rodeo held during the Dempsey-Gibbons fight at Shelby July 4, 1923.

The Flathead Indians had a large camp near the arena. People arrived by train, car, horseback, horse and buggy, and on foot—two boys ages 14 and 16 from Minneapolis walked and worked their way out to see the show. Five hundred men from Minneapolis arrived by train and requested that the show be brought to Minneapolis in the future. The show was later presented in Madison Square Garden in New York, and taken to other cities such as Ellensburg, Washington, and Tucson, Arizona.

PRIVATE HOMES, A PUBLIC CAMP GROUND, AND COLLEGE HOUSING WERE ALL ON TAP FOR THE BOZEMAN ROUNDUP CROWD

The Bozeman stampede stock included 130 head of wild longhorn steers with brass knobs on their horns for bulldogging, Brahma steers for riding, and 200 head of horses for bucking stock as well as Roman and relay races. Half of these horses came from range near White Sulphur Springs and had names such as Sky Rocket, Barrel Head and Rooster. Forty Galloway cows were brought in for the wild cow milking contest—the first time that event had been tried. Other entertainment was provided by the Indians with war dances and women's horseback races. Features included the clown, Red Sublette, roping contests and trick riding.[8]

A New Organization and Its Rodeos

In 1919, as the Bozeman Roundup developed, Eastern newspapers were heralding the start of a new organization for American cowboys. *Billboard*'s account stated:

NEW WILD WEST ORGANIZATION

———

Sponsored by Richard T. Ringling,
of Famous Circus Family,
May Revolutionize Wild West Shows

———

*Protection Is Object of
Association of American Cowboys*

———

Stampede Circuit Is To Be Formed

New York, Feb. 3.—A movement has been started here which promises to revolutionize the status of the so called Wild West show business. There was for a long time been a feeling in the minds of prominent professional cowboys, ropers, broncho busters, steer throwers and the like that all members of this fraternity of the western plains should form an organization for their mutual benefit and protection. At a meeting last Wednesday of some of the leading lights of the roping world a new order sprung into being, The Association of American Cowboys, sponsored by none other than Richard T. Ringling, of the famous circus family of that name. As is well known Mr. Ringling has a large ranch in Montana, and has for years been an ardent admirer of the genuine cowboy and his associates. Mr. Ringling has carefully watched the various roundups at Cheyenne, Tucumcari, Lethbridge. Walla Walla, Pendleton, Missoula, etc., and is of the opinion that no satisfactory results have ever yet been obtained from these exhibitions to determine the real championship caliber of the contestants.

Mr. Ringling does not intend to put out any Wild West shows, but he contemplates, with the association back of him, to form a roundup or stampede circuit, sending one troupe of boys to one point, another to another, and so on. At the end of the season those who have won "the championships" at the different celebrations would meet in a mammoth world's championship contest at Madison Square Garden or some other suitable amphitheater in New York City. As will be seen by references to our advertising columns every professional cowboy in America is invited to communicate immediately with Mr. Ringling at 1542 Broadway, New York. Mr. Ringling states that there are hundreds of towns, especially in the Middle West, that would welcome an annual roping event with open arms, and the object of the Association of American Cowboys will be primarily to keep the boys working over a properly arranged tour of the different stampedes that the organization will promote. A meeting will be held this week at which different officers will be appointed.

In October, 1923, Richard Ringling sent 10 carloads—six of horses and four of cattle—to participate in the annual Ringling Roundup in Madison Square Garden. There were

132 horses, 22 of which were saddle horses, the balance "outlaw broncs guaranteed to thrill the easterner to his heart's content." Two cars were wild steers for roping and two were for bulldogging and two were of cows and calves for wild milking contests and calf roping. A coach was attached at Harlowton for the gang of cowboys and their equipment. Loading the train was a show in itself—Ringling style.

On November 23, 1923, the *Meagher Republican* reported:

> Richard Ringling's big wild west show which has been performing at Madison Square Garden, New York city, the past ten days; had closed its engagement last Saturday night and shortly the famous riders and ropers, which include 16 Montanans, one a Helena man, Jim Galen, will be en route home.

RICHARD SENT 6 TRAINCARS OF HORSES AND 4 OF CATTLE TO THE RINGLING ROUNDUP IN MADISON SQUARE GARDEN

Jim Galen, a son of Associate Justice Albert J. Galen of the Montana Supreme court, has written home several interesting letters regarding the big event, in which he was been privileged to have a part.

There has been an average daily attendance of 40,000 spectators at the Ringling show. The entrants in the various events number 116, of which 16 are from Montana. Much of the stock used in the exhibitions are from the Montana range. Ringling, as is well known here, operates several large ranches in Meagher county. Young Jim Galen accompanied the Ringling outfit from here to New York City.

They were 13 days on the road, a stop of several days

being made at Marmouth, N.D. where a stampede was in progress. Jim won first prize in the bare-back riding in that event, the horse being a particular vicious bucker. He was unable to remain for the grand prize contest, but the judges permitted his record to be counted on for a substitute who participated but was injured.

In the Madison Square Garden show, Jim drew "Rock Creek," a horse he rode at the Montana State Fair. He was entered in the grand championship…The horse acted badly, turning a complete somersault, the cantle of the saddle catching Jim and badly bruising his hips. The judges gave him another chance, on a horse named "Danger." This horse also went over backward, injuring Galen again, but he quickly rode the horse though "not straight up."

Again, he was afforded another chance, but he was too lame and battered to continue. Under the rules, a championship riding entrant has to ride every day of the show.…

The hotels are fast filling up and the tourist camps are being taxed to capacity. A special train with cowboys and cowgirls is coming from Monte Vista, Colo.

All of the champion and expert ropers, riders, steer wrestlers and masters of the range that have competed in the wild West shows of the season have either arrived in the city or will be here on time to engage in the competitive events in the arena. The prizes are attractive, enough to induce the best in the business to be here. All of them know of the Quality of the horses that the arena manager, Johnny Mullens, has brought to the roundup this year and the most daring of them want to try out the two notorious sunfishers [twisting broncs], Glittering Gold and Prison Bar....these two recruits to the 75 bad horses now in the corrals at the stadium grounds, have never been successfully ridden, and...Glittering Gold and Prison Bar are the big attractions to the performers....

The Shriners joined the celebration in 1926, but shortly after the show, lightning struck the arena stands and fire. It was condemned and Ringling decided not to rebuild.

Johnnie Mullens was one of the cowboys who rode in the roundup. He said of Ringling:

Richard had grown up with the circus and knew nothing about cattle, sheep, or ranching in general, but he did a good job of running that ranch.

The ranchers in that section ran a lot of sheep. When the ewes were lambing it was necessary to protect them from the extreme cold, or else they would lose their lambs. As a hundred or more might be born during the night, their losses would run very high it they did not have some protection from the cold. Richard Ringling remembered that, at their headquarters in Baraboo they had several old and condemned big top tents. He sent for two of them and set them up at the ranch. The old timers said he could not get the sheep to go in them. He said, "That is no problem, if you raise the sidewalls on one side and also on the opposite side, they will go in." He tried this idea out and it worked, and so he saved his lambs. The other ranchers, seeing how well it worked asked him to order some tents for them, and so many

lambs were saved in that way. A new way of caring for
lambs was born.[8]

An old circus tent was also used as ceiling in the White
Sulphur Springs auditorium when lack of money prevented
a regular ceiling. .

In the early 1920s, Ringling had drilled for oil near Three
Forks, although the paper later reported that he had aban-
doned that well and the rig was moved to Nye where he
drilled there. In 1921, Richard, John and J.M. Kelley (the circus attorney) joined with other operators to negotiate with
the Business Council of the Crow Indian Tribe for an oil
lease on 500 acres of Crow Reservation land. Younger members on the business council were not for the scheme, and
older members supported a stronger group. In this instance,
the Ringlings were no match for the bigger oil companies
and withdrew from the competition.[9]

In 1923, he bought the Springs from Arthur Conrad for
$50,000, with the idea of building a big resort hotel.

RAINMAKER, TOO

In 1923, the *Fairfield Times* reported that Richard Ringling
"planned to make rain for Montana on a large scale. Earl T.
Vance, aviator, will be associated with Mr. Ringling in this
new enterprise, which will have its headquarters in Great
Falls."

The newspaper reported that Ringling had purchased 10
airplanes that were to be used "by professional rainmakers
in Montana's dry land farming districts" to "take various
trips to different parts of the state and by induction into
the air of electric current, positive and negative, discharge

ions from the upper wing of the machine, traveling at fast speed." The article continued that this process, developed by scientists in New York, will cause the ions to form "the nuclei of raindrops which hover over the earth in the form of clouds." A happy message, indeed, for the drought-starved farmers.

It is possible that the forestry department of the federal government, with headquarters at Missoula, will take up this latest and remarkable development of science in fighting forest fires in the western part of the state.
At the present time airplanes are being used rather extensively in Oregon for fire detection and reconnaissance, and it should be a simple matter, forestry men believe, to equip these planes with sand-carrying and electrifying devices so that when clouds are encountered over a fire the moisture may be precipitated, it possible, and thus hold down the fire until it can be corralled....

Although the news of the effort must have been happy, there is no follow-up about how effective the rain-making efforts were.
The plan did, however, present the opportunity for Paul and Jane to have their first plane ride in the biplane.

The Biering Case

Ringling was an ambitious and often aggressive businessman. On one occasion his assertive business style landed him in the middle of litigation.
The Taylors Fork Cattle Company had a 27,000-animal unit sheep ranch in Madison and Gallatin Counties, but it

did not have the livestock to make the operation profitable. Ringling entered into a lease agreement with the owners of Taylors Fork—Hans Biering and M.S. Cunningham—to run his sheep on the place

An agreement was reached. The Taylors Fork property was put into a new company, the Southern Montana Company Live Stock Co. (SMC). The company would be capitalized at $500,000 and in exchange for a 50 per cent interest, Ringling agreed to transfer 12,000 head of "good, young ewes" to SMC. Lester Work, as Ringling's sheep foreman, was in charge of the operation.

In the summer of 1921, a court later found, Ringling put 10,000 sheep at Taylors Fork. But these sheep remained in Ringling's ownership and were evidently not the sheep intended to be transferred to SMC. The wool and the lambs from these 10,000 were harvested and sold by Ringling and Work. Biering complained about the quality of the sheep, so Work culled out 4,000 and transferred the remaining animals to SMC ownership.

Ringling turned to California to buy sheep to fill in the numbers needed in Montana to fulfill his commitments and keep his extensive holdings profitable. An agreement with one C. T. Carter called for the delivery by Carter of approximately 32,500 head of lambs. By way payment, $24,800 was paid as an initial payment for 22,700 head of lambs at the rate of 1.09^1/_4$ per head. Carter delivered only 6,286 lambs and the court ruled that the Alturas Sate Bank owed Ringling and others $27,732.54 for undelivered lambs.[10]

However, without the new lambs, Ringling was short the sheep for the Southern Montana Livestock Company. In the

spring of 1922, Biering confronted Work at White Sulphur
Springs about the promise made to stock SMC with another 10,000 head of "good, young ewes." Work, as the sheep
manager for the Ringling Ranch, advised Biering that they
did not have 10,000 to put at the SMC property but that he
could arrange to put 3,000 on the place. Biering was over
a barrel because he could not stock the property any other way so he agreed to the 3,000
ewes.

RINGLING LEFT HANS BIERING AND M.S. CUNNINGHAM WITH NO PROFITS FOR TWO YEARS

Biering left the meeting with
Work to make arrangements for
trailing the sheep to SMC. When
he returned to SMC he discovered
that Work had delivered a hodgepodge of livestock—some
black faces, some white faces, many course-wool sheep and
even 150 wethers. And the 3,000 head numbered only 2,800;
Work was 200 sheep light on the count.

After another series of unfortunate financial transac-
tions—unfortunate for Biering and Cunningham—regarding the sale of the lambs in the fall of 1922, the original
owners of Taylors Fork received nothing from the herd's
production. Biering and Cunningham made no money for
two years and lost the property.

Having suffered a devastating financial loss from
their agreement with Ringling and Work, Biering and
Cunningham brought a damage suit charging Mr. Ringling with breach of contract and demanding damages in
the sum of $546,000. The title of the action, which was
pending before Judge Huntoon of Lewistown, who was
called in by Judge Ben Law of Gallatin county, is Richard

Ringling against Biering and Cunningham. The amount involved is approximately $250,000.

The trial was held in district Court in 1924. The verdict was rendered in favor of the plaintiffs in the sum of $322,480. Ringling appealed the case to the Supreme Court, but the high court affirmed the decision and the damage award against Ringling. The plaintiffs were then free to collect payment from Ringling.

Before the Biering judgment was finally affirmed, Ringling was given an opportunity to purchase about $250,000 worth of Biering and Cunningham notes which were held by the Elling State Bank. This he did and sought to offset the $322,000 judgment against himself, to the amount of the face of the notes. Biering and Cunningham pleaded that the notes didn't mean anything. That they and Kurt Elling had gone to a room in the Placer Hotel and arrived at an agreement which was put in writing, describing the notes.

Deliberation continued over the case for years. The defendants were charged in a lawsuit involving $250,000 deliberately faking a holdup to save themselves from being compelled to admit that their alleged defense had no existence, in the implication, strongly presented, in a deposition, that was taken before Charles H. Little, stenographer, to Judge W.W. Carroll and made public yesterday. The deposition was made by Joseph E. Callahan of this city. He was examined by Dan M. Kelly of Butte and M. S. Gunn of Helena, attorney for the plaintiff in the suit.

Biering continued to push for the rest of the money. The case was still in the news in 1925. As the *Helena Independent* recalled on August 4, 1943:

> The safe containing $215,000 worth of notes belonging to Richard T. Ringling, which was taken from the offices of H.D. Beatty, attorney for Mr. Ringling by the sheriff's force on Monday was returned to the attorney this morning intact. The return of the property followed a temporary stay of execution with reference of the same signed by Judge B.B. Law, after Attorney Bath had filed a petition for an order to vacate execution. The hearing will be held Monday, March 9. Attorney Bath made a return of the contents of the safe before Judge Law this morning, and after the court had signed the order for the temporary stay, the lawyer made a demand upon the sheriff for the use. It was brought back within a few minutes.
>
> The controversy concerns the damage suit brought by M. S. Cunningham and Hans Biering, stockmen, against Richard T. Ringling, millionaire showman, stockman and holder of large interests in and around White Sulphur Springs. The plaintiffs charged Mr. Ringling with wrecking their business, and demanded damages in the sum of $546,000. The trial was held in district court last summer, and a verdict rendered in favor of the plaintiffs in the sum of $322,480…, and the defendant appealed…The bonds for twice the amount of the judgment were never filed, and last Friday attorneys for the plaintiffs learned of the promissory notes amounting to $215,000 belonging to Ringling being in possession of H.D. Bath, attorney for Ringling. An exe-

cution on the judgment was asked and the sheriff was ordered to attach the notes. When the officers arrived at the lawyer's office they were informed that the notes were in the safe, along with personal possessions of the attorney.

That the defendants in a lawsuit involving $250,000 deliberately faked a holdup to save themselves from being compelled to admit that their alleged defense had no existence, in the implication, strongly presented, in a deposition, that was taken before Charles H. Little, stenographer, to Judge W.W. Carroll and made public yesterday. The deposition was made by Joseph E. Callahan of this city. He was examined by Dan M. Kelly of Butte and M. S. Gunn of Helena, attorney for the plaintiff in the suit.

The surrounding circumstances are as follows: Ringling engaged in the cattle and sheep raising business with Biering and Cunningham. Differences arise. Ringling was sued for breach of contract. They were awarded $322,480.

BIERING AND CUNNINGHAM CLAIMED THAT RINGLING AND WORK STAGED A FAKE BURGLARY TO EVADE THE LAW

Counsel for Biering and Cunningham then stated that the original agreement had been lost but that they had a copy of the original and that the copy is more than seven years old. Judge Law ordered them to produce the copy.

Karl Elling had denied that any such agreement had ever been made.

Litigation continued for years. As late as 1943, the case was in court as Aubrey Ringling sought to negate the debt by claiming that Biering, as a Danish citizen should have obtained a license before contracting business. The court ruled that even an alien enemy could not be deprived of his day in court. Biering's attorneys said there was about $47,000 still at stake in addition to many years of interest.

In 1929, Ringling bought 51,213 acres of Northern Pacific land situated on west side of Gallatin River to be used for summer range for sheep. The area was checker-boarded, meaning alternate sections were owned by the forest reserve. Exchange was made, at which the sections, alternating with Ringling's recent purchases and part of the forest reserve, was exchanged for a railroad checkerboard in another part of the forest. When that was completed Ringling purchased the even numbered sections, thereby doubling the present holdings in Gallatin County.

Ringling also invested in commercial and residential property in the city of Bozeman in 1922 when he built the rodeo stands. Aubrey sold this property in 1934 for back taxes.[11]

FAMILY CHANGES

Richard's mother died in 1930 and his sister Marjorie moved to Montana.

Marjorie was educated at Holton Arms School, Washington D.C., and Bronson School in Manhattan, and was attending college in Arizona when her mother died there in 1930.

She was counted in the census in 1930 in White Sulphur Springs with brother Richard, and was staying at the Montana Ranch when her brother died. She went on to New York to Uncle John, and studied music in 1933 at the American Conservatory, in Fontainebleau, France. She was living in New York when she met and married Jacob Javits in 1933.

Javits attended Columbia University and the New York University Law School (J.D. 1926) He joined brother Benjamin Javits as partner to form the Javits and Javits Law firm. The brothers specialized in bankruptcy and minority stockholders suits and became quite successful. Javits served as a U.S. Senator from 1957 to 1981.

Marjorie and Javits were divorced in 1936. That was the same year that John Ringling, his health and fortune breaking as the circus struggled through the Depression, died.

RICHARD AND AUBREY, 1931

Over the years, Aubrey was faced with the ups and downs of their fortune. Along with the financial problems, Richard's health continued a problem. On May 13 of 1931, two years into the Great Depression, Richard was in the East working with the circus, trying to find financing for his own depleted fortune and checking in with doctors. He hadn't lost his flair for writing or his sense of humor, though things looked dour for the Montana rancher. He wrote to Aubrey about his visit with doctors.

…We now continue with the Physical hour on how to keep fit. First rush from Montana to New York on dogs that can hardly carry you not sleeping at all kidding yourself by trying to keep going on Montana moon and after that runs out on the (Bonded stuff just off the boat) which is worse. Have feet examined getting appliances to wear and much rough and painful mauling then advice to go to Florida for rest on account run down condition, walk in loose sand with lots of massage. Take Nemo [Nemo the Clown] along for massage and to take care of place and no doubt to your surprise he has done well in both positions...

"...having foot treatment by a man who is so gentle I called him Tarzan."

From New York, Ringling reported:

...urine was examined and it seems everything was found in it except urine and the Doctor thought there must be stones in my Kidneys. From there I went to Sarasota where I had another examination and Doctor thought I must have stones. By this time I thought perhaps I might be turning into a rock pile. Then to Milton where teeth were suggested as a possible source of infection; but x-rays disproved of this theory and was put on one of those fresh vegetable diets. This of course is hard to follow in Florida as the restaurants refuse to serve them altho they are literally surrounded by them. I then went to Sarasota to be examined by Dr. Kennedy who thought it might be the appendix, as you know he has had a yen for that appendix for some time. By this time I was becoming irked to say the least. In fact at times I was accused of exhibiting certain marked and obvious signs of peevishness. I then asked the good doctor if he thought that throughout the breadth of Sarasota enough gentlemen of the surgical and medical professions, together with the proper tools and equipment to perform an exploratory operation to determine whether I had stones in my kidneys or if it was the result of wearing camelhair underwear in my early youth that was the cause of the present disturbance and if there was a decent xray machine in town or did they fool the public by shooting sparks over a Brownie Kodak? Did they have a room with a bath in the hospital? Were the nurses attractive and more or less reasonable, in case upon convalescing, one should become slightly amorous?

He replied with some heat that he himself being forced to admit he was no slouch as a surgeon and that he himself had tools and equipment that would no doubt knock my eye out and that he with the assistance of one Medico dubbed Metzler could perform the operation. That Dr. Wilson was one of the finest anesthetists in the country excelled by none and equaled by few, that the exray equipment at the Sarasota Hospital was of the best and the operator competent. That while there were no rooms with bath at the hospital, the baths were in close proximity to the rooms but that I need not start worrying about that as I would not be using them anyway. That as far as there nurses were concerned, in his opinion they need not take a back seat from any, that I need not worry myself on that score either, as that when he got thru with me I would be safe in the midst of a Cooch Dance Convention....

I informed the doctor that he also need have no worry regarding the anesthetist, that while I did not doubt his

> HIS DOCTORS ACCUSED RICHARD OF "EXHIBITING CERTAIN MARKED AND OBVIOUS SIGNS OF PEEVISHNESS," AS HE WROTE TO AUBREY

ability that I cared for no ether or chloroform, that three injections of Novocain at the base of the spine aided by the internal consumption of six grains of sodium ananol would suffice to start the operation and that after the second hour quarter grain injections of codeine could be given that I wished to remain awake while persons were operating in the vicinity of certain parts of my anatomy and that my distrust of Crackers was well known anyhow that if this were oke with him I wished to proceed with the utmost of dispatch and get the damned business over with. So I was ordered to proceed to the Hospital the following evening and await the dawn which I did.

There is no need of going into the details of the operation itself as I well know persons are inclined to exaggerate when narrating in relation to their experiences undergoing operations. In this they make tyro fibbers out of fishermen. I will simply state that the waving of electric lights around the inside of one's bladder and the other manipulations incumbent to the making of a good complete cystoscopic examination are far from pleasant and that it was at last determined that there were no stones in my kidneys but that adhesions emanating from my appendix were causing the trouble and that [both adhesions and appendix] should be removed[,] but that inasmuch as I would not stand for general anesthesia and that he would operate in no other manner[,] that he had already been working on me for four hours and would not operate any [other] way[,] that he was tired and hungry going to quit and go home to lunch. That as far as he was concerned I could have the truculent appendix and adhesions removed in Honkong, Hastings or Hell with or without pain easing potions by some butcher who would not mind being told how to go about his own business. As he left I was trundled off to bed. In due time I left the hospital in possession of a large number of xray files showing that someday I may need the appendix operation but that the renal organs are free from pebbles.

Things physical went along pretty well until ten days ago when I came down and was laid low with a combined attack of the adhesion-appendix combination, stacis and nephritis from which I am just recovering. In fact today is my second day out since the attack. I will use this as an alibi for not having the letter promised…The shows are doing well and I am sure if we can wiggle thru the next forty days everything will be all right. If this comes true and I hope and pray it does I intend to come out there and take a good rest. I need it."
Days later, Richard reported more healing in another letter to Aubrey:

AS HIS HEALTH DECLINED, RICHARD STILL MADE LIGHT OF PROBLEMS IN LETTERS HOME

Dear Aubrey, Just a note to let you know I deposited one thousand dollars to your account today…and five hundred dollars to Olga…

…My underground police operative T99 informs me Lester Work fired a salvo in the honor and direction of a Medico he accused of undue familiarity with Sugar, but not being well versed in the art of marksmanship the results proved negligible.

I surely would like to get to Montana for awhile but guess I will have to stay here for some time yet rooting around hither and yon in hopes of bringing a shekel or two to the surface. The bankers are so tight here they could wade thru rivers with both arms full of eels and never lose a one. However there is where the money is and I believe someone one remarked that "You can't get it where it aint."

I am feeling much better than when I last wrote you and the Doctor has lessened the stringency of my diet to such an extent that limiting myself to the prescribed foods has ceased to be much of a hardship. However, I am not permitted the use of bread, which is hell when a beaker of Gravy is on deck.

If you see Glen Roscoe ask him to write me showing the present status of the manifold company as I think I might be able to do something with it while here.

I have been busier all day than an armless wonder with the crabs so will close and get something to eat…
Love Rick[12]

On September 4, 1931, the *Meagher Republican* reported that Richard and his sister Marjorie had been to Great Falls to attend the fair and visit friends. Richard, at the time, was in good health, vigorous, and lively.

He had retired at midnight, and Monday morning talked to Mrs. Ringling and he was apparently in good health. His daughter Jane talked to him shortly before ten o'clock, when he said he would bath and be downstairs later. When the family called him for lunch the body was found on the floor clad in his bathrobe.

According to the paper, Richard Ringling had come to White Sulphur Springs to manage "the big ranch interests of his uncle, John Ringling, who a few years previously had made heavy investments here in the railroad and livestock business." Richard was portrayed as a pillar of the community, and "one of the finest ranchers in the Northwest."

His obituary in the *Meagher Republican* on September 4, 1931, noted:

He devoted himself to farming and ranching, running both cattle and sheep and to dairying. He had at the time of his death a fine herd of purebred Hereford stock, and large bands of sheep and herds of cattle running here and on his property on the upper Madison. It is said his land holding aggregate 200,000 acres of deeded land...His dairy interests here were also great, and besides having the west's finest herd of Holstein cattle, built here the largest dairy barn west of the Mississippi. His business interests outside of the circuses were varied, including large land holding on the west coast of Florida. He is also reported to have important mine ventures.

With John Ringling and the Chas. Ringling estate, he was a partner in the Ringling-Barnum and Bailey circus and the other groups of circuses acquired later. Listed among the Ringling owned shows are the Barnes, Sells-Floto, Forepaugh and other circus shows that tour the west. Mr. Ringling is also reported to be heavily interested in the Madison Square Garden venture.

Mr. Ringling was a Mason, a member of Algeria

temple of the Shrine, and of several hunting clubs. He took an active interest in state politics, and was a large contributor to Republican campaign funds. He was state committeeman from this county."

With all that, he was also very overextended financially and although his widow, Aubrey, was left with large assets, she was also saddled with a great deal of debt. Along with the agricultural interests, she had a one-third ownership of the Ringling Brothers Circus. The business took much of her time, and her children became more self-sufficient.

YEARS OF THE GREAT DEPRESSION

When Richard died, the country was deep in the Great Depression, and the West in a drought. As his son, Paul, remembered,

> ...'27 was one of the real wet years...I remember it seemed like it rained every day...the drought started in the '30's and then '31, '32, '33 were really the "pits" in Montana and agriculture...it was dry and the prices were just in the tank. I can remember those, I can remember that it was either the Fall of '31 or '32 that lambs brought 2 cents, wool brought 8 cents a pound and a good calf brought 12 dollars a head and some people in at White Sulphur didn't think that 12 dollars were enough for their calves and sent them to Sioux City and got 8 dollars a head for them after they paid the freight.[13]

The *Meagher County Republican* reported in 1931:

[Richard] had at the time of his death a fine herd of purebred Hereford stock, and large bands of sheep and herds of cattle, running here and on his property on the upper Madison. It is said his land holdings aggregate 200,000 acres of deeded land, one of the greatest ranches in the northwest. His dairy interests here were also great, and besides having the west's finest…Holstein cattle, built here the largest dairy barn west of the Mississippi. His business interests outside of the circuses were varied, including large land holding on the west coast of Florida. He is also reported to have important mine ventures.

Many of the investments that Richard had made were disastrous in the business climate of the 1930s. He had gone through several million dollars, and the major asset now was his one-third interest in the Combined Shows. To help Aubrey, in her distress, Uncle John [Ringling] squeezed some money for her out of the hard-pressed circus. As a result, her children were sent some years to private schools, although after spending time in a military school in the East, Paul finished his high school in Livingston, staying at the Murray Hotel and boarding with a Mrs. Ebert. Mable spent some time traveling with the circus as an equestrian, but Jane chose to stay in Montana.

AUBREY AND THE CIRCUS

Following Richard's death in 1931, Aubrey also chose to take an active part as a circus vice president and traveled with the circus, often taking her children. The girls were along more often than Paul, who preferred life on the ranch.

In 1935, Aubrey told the *New York Sun* and the home town paper in White Sulphur Springs about her life as part of the circus family.

When she was 18, she rode eighteen miles in a buckboard with a...crowd of young people to see Ringling Brothers Circus at Lewistown, never dreaming that in a couple of years she would become a part of the circus world or that she herself would be a third owner and vice president of the largest circus in the world. Or that she would be worrying for fear that her own little girls would run away and join the circus.

Mrs. Ringling, a rather slight looking vivacious little woman with keen, merry, gray eyes, recalled those days today at the Ringling Brothers–Barnum and Bailey Circus in Madison Square Garden. In addition to her interest in the circus management, she owns and operates a 45,000 acre ranch at White Sulphur Springs, and sent 211,000 pounds of wool to market last year. She has 1,000 head of cattle and 19,000 sheep, and employs a whole flock of cowboys, among them her own son, Paul, now in junior college.

...Her two little daughters, Jane 14, and Mable 11, both are in school in New York—when they aren't at the circus. It's never lost its attractiveness for them. Mrs. Ringling is wondering how in the world she's going to keep them from joining up some day. Both are trick riders and ropers, and they think the cowboy acts in the circus just about the grandest thing on earth...

...(Richard) came to White Sulphur Springs with the idea of buying a ranch to raise horses.

…"When Mr. Ringling came to town," said Mrs. Ringling, "naturally I couldn't help meeting him. There are only 574 people in our town, and you can't very well miss anybody. We met and liked each other, and before we knew it we were married. Mr. Ringling bought the big ranch, and I immediately became a ranch woman. That is, we commuted between ranch and circus.

"I think it was the second year I was married that we went on the road with the circus during the summer, I traveled right along, eating in the cook tent with all the others, and getting acquainted with everybody. You can imagine what a thrilling experience for a girl who had never been anywhere or seen anything—outside of the Rocky Mountains."

Both of Richard and Aubrey's daughters were accomplished riders. Here, Jane shows English style.

"How did I spend the summer last year?" she asked. "Well, if you really want to know, I spent most of actually hauling things around in a truck. My children were active cow hands, and I was a truck driver, hauling men and supplies to strategic points all over the ranch. Forty-five thousand acres is quite a territory, you know, and to get 19,000 sheep sheared, and all those beeves to market, keeps you stepping. Managing a ranch these days, at a profit, is no child's play. But I love it."

This winter she came to New York to put the children in school. Everything went well until the circus came to town. Jane and Mabel can be found there when they can't be found anywhere else. They know all of the 1,800 persons connected with it, and Jane has autographs of nearly all of them. And both little girls insist they want to join up.

Mrs. Ringling herself is going on the road with the circus for part of the summer. She will send her son, Paul [then only fifteen], to the ranch to look after things for a time. He's very competent, she says.

So are the daughters, both of whom can lasso a steer or a horse when necessary. For that matter, so can Mrs. Ringling herself. She could perform creditably in the Wild West section of the circus, if she had a mind to, but feels it's not the place for her, even if she had time.

"I know it would be fun," she said today, her eyes sparkling merrily, "but if I did, Jane and Mabel would be with the circus before the month is over. And after all, I do have other plans for them. I'd rather they'd marry a nice ranchman, or even just a plain cowboy. Our country is grand. I love it. Much better than any of your cities, better even than the circus, I regret to say. I don't think my son is quite as daft over the circus as the girls are. He's a real rancher, I think.[14]

Aubrey embarked on many years of putting the family's personal affairs into order, work with the circus as a one-third owner, and raise a family. Paul was 12, Mable 7, and Jane 10. Paul said,

AUBREY SAID "MANAGING A RANCH THESE DAYS, AT A PROFIT, IS NO CHILD'S PLAY. BUT I LOVE IT."

...my mother probated the estate from 1931 to 1947. It was a financial disaster...a good way to describe it[,] and my mother really did a remarkable job of coming out right sides up with all the lawsuits and the things that were involved. The claims...my mother of course was raised in White Sulfur Springs...the sheriff was a good friend of my mother's... so the sheriff would call my mother and tell her that I have these papers to serve...my mother would go down to Ringling, hop on the train and she was gone and he just couldn't find her.[15]

Aubrey took an active part in the running of the circus, taking part in the financial and management decisions. Two years after Richard's death Aubrey married Eugene Cardonyi, the Hungarian-born trust officer of the Irving Trust Company. This marriage was short lived. According to circus legend, Cardonyi sought to speak for his wife during a business meeting. Aubrey, without a word, returned to their

THREE RINGLINGS IN MONTANA

hotel and personally chucked all of the gentleman's effects into the hall. They later divorced.

Ten years later, Aubrey married James Haley, who had been associated with the circus in several capacities over the years. He was working as an accountant for John Ringling and later served as general manager of John's estate. He chose to stay with the circus. After Aubrey and Haley married in 1942, they voted their stock together.

Haley served as a member of the Florida House of Representatives from 1949 to 1952 and was elected to Congress, serving from 1959 until 1977.

The year that Aubrey remarried for the second time, in 1946, she sold the home in White Sulphur Springs to Robert and Thelma Johnson for $17,500.

Aubrey and Haley continued to live in Florida and Washington, although Aubrey was visiting in Montana with her daughter, Mrs. Floyd Shellhamer, when she died in 1976 at age 81.

Paul Ringling had run the ranch after his return from military service. He had the opportunity to work for the circus, but opted to run the ranch instead. When Aubrey decided to sell the Montana property in 1949, Paul and Althea were able to borrow the money to finance 25,000 acres and establish their own ranch.

1. Henry Ringling North and Alden Hatch, *The Circus Kings* (Garden City, NY: Doubleday & Company, 1960).
2. Vivian A. Paladin, "Conversations with Boo" (Montana Episodes), *Montana: The Magazine of Western History* (Autumn 1980) 30:3, 52-58.
3. Landon Jones, "Babe in the Woods: F. Scott Fitzgerald's Unlikely Summer in Montana," *Montana: The Magazine of Western History*, 57:3 (Autumn 2007).
4. Theresa Buckingham, *The Old Party in the Feathered Shawl* (White Sulphur Springs, MT: Meagher County News, 1980), 38-41.
5. Phyllis Smith, *Bozeman and Gallatin Valley: A History* (Helena, MT: Two Dot Press, 1996), 241.
6. Ibid.
7. Information courtesy of Laura Potter McMillan, John's daughter.
8. Mullens family papers.
9. David C. Weeks, *Ringling: The Florida Years, 1911-1930* (Gainesville: University of Florida Press, 1993), 234-5.
10. Bierling v. Ringling, 74 Mont. 176240 P. 829 (1922).
11. Deed Record 65, Gallatin County Deed records, Bozeman, Montana.
12. Ringling family papers.
13. Paul Ringling interview by Brian Shovers, February 2002.
14. *Meagher County News*, May 15, 1935.
15. Paul Ringling interview.

Aubrey Ringling Haley with Mabel, Paul, and Jane in 1953.

CIRCUS HEIR, RANCHER & LEGISLATOR

PAUL RINGLING (1920–)

BORN IN NEW YORK CITY to Richard and Aubrey Ringling on April 21, 1920, Paul Ringling spent childhood winters on Long Island, New York, and in Sarasota, Florida, where the circus by then wintered, and summers on the family ranch in White Sulphur Springs, Montana, traveling back and forth by the Milwaukee Railway. When they were in New York, Paul was surrounded by the circus world of his grandfather and his great-uncles. At times, Paul remembered, his baby sitter had been Nemo the

Clown. What he longed for, however, was Montana. The *Butte Miner* reported in 1924 that five-year-old Paul considered riding in Central Park too much like a "dude trick" and was anxious to get back to Montana and ride like a gentleman.

> When the circus comes to town along in the spring, a dashing horse act, original in every detail, may be seen in the center ring, if the boyhood wishes of a future owner of the big show comes to pass.
> Already Paul T. Ringling, the five-year old great nephew of John and Charles, and the son of Richard. T. whose father was one of the...brothers who founded the circus that bears their name, has expressed that desire...
> Paul doesn't care much for elephants and other wild beasts. He is all for horses... Paul looks forward to the time he can go with the big show.[1]

Paul worked during the summers and some winters at the Birch Creek Ranch west of White Sulphur Springs, which was managed by Dick Collins, who went on to manage the Bozeman Stampede. From the time he was four, Paul rode a Shetland pony on the Ringling ranch, and started riding a quarter horse at the age of seven. Paul became life-long friends with George Culler, one of the sons in the Culler family who had a mountain ranch farther west up the main Birch Creek. In an interview with Brian Shovers of the Montana Historical Society, Paul recalled the amazing freedom of movement he had in the late 1920s when, from the age of nine until he was thirteen, he traveled by horseback from the Birch Creek Ranch to Culler's Ranch:

Jane and Paul

Jane and Mabel

We had more freedom on the ranch when we were on horseback and did everything and rode everywhere. There were no telephones and roads and things were more primitive and a lot of work was done by horses. Nobody ever knew or, they didn't know if I got there or I didn't get there and I may be up at Culler's for a week or maybe longer. Then, we had a cow camp south of White Sulphur Springs, between there and Ringling, George and I would leave his folks' place horseback and ride to that cow camp and stay there maybe a week or maybe longer. His folks would assume we got there and the people at Birch Creek...they hadn't seen me for two weeks or more...but we rode all over that country and hunted and fished. We lived a life that I don't think you could really do now.[2]

Paul, his parents and his sisters Mable and Jane, lived in White Sulphur in the large Parberry House, with a coal stoves and a "stoker furnace" that Paul had the responsibility to keep filled with coal. He recounted an amiable small-town childhood with games of kick-the-can, and Fox and Goose in the winter, as well as skating and sledding. He was colorblind so in school, when he had to color a turkey at Thanksgiving, "he didn't know what the colors were on those crayons till [he] was able to read." He loved history and enjoyed reading Will James and Albert Payson Terhune, who was famous for his Lad stories about rough-coat collies.

Paul remembered the large dairy barn and creamery with its standard concrete floor, where they milked cows three times a day, tested the milk, and produced Castle Mountain Gold butter that was served on the Milwaukee Railroad. He also remembered when the barn, next to their home, burned in 1932. "I owned a canary then," Ringling recalled. "He was upside with his feet in the air from the smoke."[3]

His childhood idyll came to an end when his father Richard died on September 4, 1931, when Paul was eleven

Paul worked in a ticket wagon like this one.

years of age. As Paul observed that after his father's death, after that point, "we didn't have much of a family life." Paul, Jane, and Mable were sent away to school while his mother struggled to probate the estate: Paul went to the New York Military Academy at Cornwall on Hudson for two years of his high school where he was in the cavalry unit from 1931 to 1933. Paul graduated from high school in 1937 in Livingston, Montana, where he lived at the Murray Hotel and boarded with a Mrs. Ebert, who "made some of the best upside-down cake I ever ate in my life."[5]

Jane and Mable went off to boarding schools, with intermittent stays in White Sulphur Springs. His mother traveled back and forth from Montana to New York and Florida from 1931 to 1947 while the estate of Richard Ringling was in probate. The estate, Paul observed, was a "financial disaster" but he noted that his mother did a "remarkable job of coming out right side up" with all the claims that were against it.

Then, in true Ringling fashion, Paul went to work for the Ringling Circus, as had his father and his uncles before him. He started out as a ticket taker—charged with the important task of not only selling and taking tickets, but making sure that the number of tickets sold matched the amount of money taken in at each show. Paul worked five seasons for the circus, from 1937 to 1941.

When he worked as a ticket taker, Paul said he rode in the squadron car or the first section, going to work at 3:30 in the morning after a hearty breakfast of bacon, hot cakes, sausage at 6:30. Dinner was held at noon and formal with long tables covered with tablecloths and waiters. "We had supper at 4:30 and fed 1,200 people a day, 3 times a day. The animals were fed hay and grain; the tigers were fed meat, except on Sunday, when they got milk and eggs." The circus moved every day while it was "trouping," except for two-day stays in New York, Boston, San Francisco, Los Angeles, and a five-day stay in Chicago. When they had an overnight stay in a city, Paul said, one or two of the circus members would secure a hotel room, then the rest would file through to take baths. The troupe

IN THE CIRCUS, PAUL WENT TO WORK AT 3:30 A.M., PAUSING FOR A HOT BREAKFAST AT 6:30.

had its own doctor and veterinarian. Laundry was dropped off at a cleaner in one town and when it was cleaned, it was shipped ahead to the next stop by rail express.

In June 1938, the circus season lasted just 10 weeks and closed early in Scranton, Pennsylvania, because of a five-day strike there that cost the Ringling Bros. and Barnum & Bailey Combined Shows $250,000. The show was losing $440,000 a week before the strike. Engagements had to be canceled. However, the circus came back in 1939 to a great year.

Paul returned to White Sulphur Springs to spend the summer with his friend, George Culler. Culler's father had died and his mother lost part of the ranch, so Paul helped with the work at Culler's until fall, when he threshed grain for Oscar Olsen. He spent two quarters at the University of Montana–Missoula. Paul returned to the circus in 1939 and when the season ended, he wintered with them in Sarasota, doing winter chores for the circus.

During the years he traveled with the circus, the Ringling Brothers Circus visited Montana in 1939 and 1941. The circus spent one half-day each in Helena, Butte, and Missoula. In Montana, he visited every town's downtown to set up advance posters and advertising and many of the tickets were sold at the large department stories, such as Fligelman's in Helena and the Mercantile in Missoula.

After his years as a ticket seller, he was promoted to the set-up crew responsible for putting up the Big Top, and spotting wagons. The last year he worked in outdoor advertising. By this point, he was married, and he and his young wife, Althea, traveled together weeks ahead of the circus trains setting up outdoor advertising—the billboards, posters, and newspaper advertising, as well as securing licenses for the show grounds and the arrival parade. The advertising was still what Jerry Apps called in his book *Ringlingville* "blatant hyperbole," as it had been in a 1902 ad advertising a giraffe that was the "only giraffe known to exist in the entire world. $20,000 was the price he cost....the last, the only one, the single sole and lovely survivor of a once numerous race."[6]

Paul reported it was great fun traveling with the circus: the camaraderie, working with the crews, living in close quarters on the Pullman cars. He noted that it was quite an adjustment when, later in his life, he had to adjust to living in more isolated circumstances on his ranch in White Sulphur Springs.

THE RINGLING SISTERS

When the family was split apart after Richard Ringling's death, Paul's sister, Jane, who was born on March 26, 1921, attended Annie Wright Seminary in Tacoma, Washington, until approximately 1938, and in 1939, graduated from White Sulphur Springs high school. She was never interested in participating in the Ringling circus, although she and Mable traveled with their mother after their father died.

In 1950, she married a man named Lloyd Shelhamer, a cowboy and rodeo rider. They had six children: Renee, Sharon, Shelley, Susan, John, and Linda. At that point, Shelhamer gave up rodeoing. With his father, Lloyd raised race horses. In 1954, Jane and Lloyd built the Beaumont Racetrack and Night Club in Belgrade, Montana, which they ran through 1964. They introduced horse racing to many family and friends who went on to make racing a career.

In 1957, they founded United Tote Company, which provided betting equipment for race tracks in Montana and in nearby states. After developing a computerized system in 1979, United Tote grew rapidly to become a major international supplier with more than 130 customers, among them Churchill Downs in Kentucky. Lloyd also managed racetracks, directed the Thoroughbred Racing Association and received a lifetime achievement award from the Quarter Horse Racing Association in 1995.

Mable Ellen Ringling was born on March 10, 1924, in New York, New York, and died on May 31, 2004, in Princeton, Mercer, Missouri.

She attended the Ursuline Academy in Great Falls for a couple of years beginning when she was about nine years old.

Mable traveled with her mother while Aubrey worked with the Ringling Circus as vice president. She was a trouper at nine, spending summers at the Montana Ranch or traveling with the circus.

As a child, Mable had performed in circus spot acts—riding elephants and ponies—and riding as a fairy princess buggy driver. She secretly "worked with the cats" until her stepfather, James Haley, threatened to fire the leopard trainers for allowing her to do this. Later she became a horse trainer and equestrian, putting her horses through intricate routines, dressed in costumes so laden with sequins and heavy material, she needed help mounting.

Mable is an equestrienne and appeared in riding numbers with the circus last year but her show career ended abruptly when her mother nipped a romance with one of the show's elephant trainers by escorting her to the family home in White Sulphur Springs. (*Billboard,* November 26, 1949)

Mable "retired" when Aubrey sold her interest in the circus.

In an article in *Montana Magazine* for September-October 1983, Mable told of some of the life of the circus.

Wash day for the circus crew was almost a primitive chore. Without benefit of modern Laundromats, clothing was scrubbed in a water bucket, then dried on a length of clothesline strung between the tent ropes. And lacking a beauty parlor on the premise, we washed our hair in the buckets too.

The first show of the season opened in April in Madison Square Garden, then the circus would move on to the Boston Gardens. Philadelphia got third billings, the first under

PERFORMER HYGIENE WAS BUCKET-BASED DURING MABLE'S TIME WITH THE CIRCUS

the Big Top each year, because the tents were made in the city and each year a new one was required. After seven months of being put up and down, the tents would be worn out...

Contracting a vacant lot and erecting "tent city" was a major, orchestrated job. The mammoth "big top" was 450 feet long, 200 feet wide and took more than 20 tons of canvas or 74,000 yards. There were usually more than 40 other tents set up for each performance, and it took eight giant diesel plants to furnish 168,000 watts of power to keep everything running smoothly.

About 1,600 people traveled in a 100-car railroad caravan during circus time. The dining room, thought to be the largest traveling restaurant in the world, was dubbed the Hotel Ringling.

Keeping the crew, performers and staff fed three times a day from a menu was a giant feat also. An average daily grocery list was something like this—226 dozen eggs, 2,470 pounds of fresh meat, 2,220 loaves of bread, and if pancakes were on the menu, the air was literally filled with "tumbling cakes."

Mable married Russell A. Anderson on November 12, 1949, in Great Falls, Montana. A graduate of Devils Lake High School in North Dakota, Anderson was in the U.S. Navy until 1946, when he attended a trade school in Wahpeton, North Dakota. Mable and Russell bought a 1,700-acre ranch in southwestern Montana. He served as a Madison County commissioner, and was a member of the Masonic Lodge. He also obtained his pilot's license, and built and flew his own helicopter.

Russell and Mable divorced in 1980, and their 3,200-acre ranch was sold. Russell moved to Butte where he developed, owned and operated a number of businesses including R & J Amusements, The Carousel, Sportsman Bar, and owned additional commercial properties. He also owned the Blue Moon Cafe and Bar in Twin Bridges, and partnered in land development in western Montana.

Mable later had a farm in Missouri and became an active 4-H leader. She died May 31, 2004, in Mercer, Missouri.

• • •

PAUL AND ALTHEA: PARTNERS IN EVERYTHING

Paul Ringling met his wife-to-be in White Sulphur Springs when they were in the eighth grade and, he reported, they "got serious about each other" when they were sixteen. Althea Shearer grew up and attended school in White Sulphur Springs, but she was born on a homestead at Sixteen Mile, Montana, a station on the Milwaukee Railway. Shortly after Paul graduated from high school in Livingston, he married Althea, on December 18, 1940. He later described as his "partner in everything." They married in a church, with good friends who owned a saddle shop in Livingston serving as witnesses, "just the four of us there when we were married." For a honeymoon, they drove their 1934 Ford Coupe to Cooke City, on to Bozeman, then home to White Sulphur Springs, where, on New Year's Eve, the town had a chivaree for them.

Althea Ringling

My aunt came down and told us we better get out of town because they were going to have a chivaree for us...but there's no use, we can't escape...so they gathered us up and it was cold that night and the sheriff, Mike Bergan, had the team and an old stage coach and they rolled us up and down White Sulfur Springs in the stage coach that New Year's Eve.[7]

In 1939, Paul and Althea traveled for a year with the circus, as Paul worked as an advance man. It was a time he recalled fondly, traveling with his new bride from town to town in their 1934 Ford coupe "with the door that opened to the front, a classic."[8]

From Advance Man to Radio Operator

By the time the United State entered the war in Europe in 1941, the young Ringlings had returned to Montana and, by the next spring, the draft board told Ringling he qualified for an agricultural deferment, but he chose to volunteer in September 1942 anyway.

After basic training at Fort Douglas in Salt Lake City, in

Paul Ringling in his 90s

fall 1942, Ringling was sent to Signal Corps at Camp Kohler and then to Kansas City where he was trained as a high speed radio operator. He worked as a radio operator in a counterintelligence unit in North Africa, in Castellano, Marseille, and then in northern Italy. "It was a super secret outfit," Ringling said, describing his work as an intercept operator. Their mission was tracking the Luftwaffe, German air force, and

as a radio operator I had to be able to tell German signals—German air signals from all the other German stuff. Then you had to be able to tell whether it was a plane to the ground or ground to the plane and they were super security conscious.

Ringling's outfit was moved to Italy and headquartered at Castellano. When the war was over in Europe, they were scheduled to move on to the South Pacific, but when the bombs were dropped in Japan, orders were changed. "Nine days later," Paul said, "the troops were sent from Naples to Newport News, Virginia." Ringling spent two and a half years in the service before he returned home in August 1945 for a leave of ninety days. While Paul was in the army, Althea went to Butte Business School and went to work at Montana Agricultural College in Bozeman. When Paul returned, she quit her job and the two traveled to Lake McDonald Lodge, rented a cabin, and, in Paul's words, "got reacquainted."

When he was discharged in fall 1945, Ringling went to the Montana Agricultural College on the G.I. bill, and they lived in what Paul describes as "a little walkup thing" on Babcock in Bozeman. In the spring, he planned to return to the circus to work in the advertising department, but the circus by then was, as Paul described, "a family mess." He and Althea discussed it, and after they had been separated so long, and with their first child on the way, they weren't sure that the circus life was the best option for them. Paul recalled that their thinking was that the circus would "have another change in management and I'll be out on the road, so I went back to the ranch in White Sulphur."

HEREFORDS ON WHITE TAIL CREEK

From 1946 to 1949, Paul managed the Ringling Ranch on the Smith River, running both sheep and cattle. Aubrey sold her circus shares in 1947, and in 1949, she decided to sell the ranch. Paul and Althea bought 25,000 acres of the ranch "with no money and a lot of credit" and started their own spread. The main part of the ranch was north of White Sulphur Springs, between Whitetail Creek and Sheep Creek, with the ranch headquarters on White Tail Creek. In a season, they would put up about 500 tons of hay, all irrigated, and get a second cutting of alfalfa, and they were able to graze cattle in the summer. One summer they sold close to one thousand yearlings. But that first year on the ranch was memorable because of the heavy snowfall that started in January, which made White Sulphur Springs even more isolated than ever from the rest of the world.

Everything was closed—the railroad, the highways— it got down to 40 degrees below zero and a terrific snowfall that winter and the big snow started in January…So I rode down….we had everything at the ranch…staples, a milk cow, and fed with a team so you didn't have to go to town for anything. I rode horseback from White Sulfur Springs down to that one ranch that winter…that was 30 miles and I had a neighbor about half way and I used two saddle horses and left one at his place and he'd take care of my saddle horse and I'd ride on…and I made way better time on horseback.

I'd pass people, rode by people stuck and everything…but that's a winter you can remember. They finally brought big rotary plows in from the air base to help clean the roads out into White Sulphur that winter and the railroad was plugged and the highways were all closed.

When Paul and Althea took over, they ran only cattle on cow/calf pairs on a yearly basis, then later raised yearlings and bought calves. Paul said he first had a mixture of shorthorn Hereford cross cattle, then gradually switched over to Black Angus.

PAUL PREFERRED RAISING BLACK ANGUS CATTLE

I just like the Angus cattle. I think the mothers are good mothers, they're good rustlers. When it's snowy and cold, they are out trying to make their own way and not standing down bawling for some hay....and they obviously sell well.

The Ringlings sold some of their cattle through order buyers, the remainder they shipped to the auction yards, using the Ringling Railroad that shipped to Ringling. There the cattle were transferred onto the Milwaukee Railway, and that line traveled on to Butte.

Paul said some of the best grasses that they had in White Sulphur Springs were the Idaho fescue, a good range grass, then the shorter buffalo grass, brome grasses, and in the meadows timothy and Alsace, and wild hay. There was also wild rye, rough fescue, but he noted that range horses, "hundreds of range horses" that were "homesteaders' horses that had been turned loose and there were hundreds of those...."

During this time, Paul and Althea's children were born: Rick in 1946, Ann in 1948, and Paul Jr., always called "Rock," in 1952. Rock arrived on the 6th of September in the middle of a rainstorm and Paul remembered calling the doctor in Bozeman to tell him they were on their way, and then driving in the pouring rain "from White Sulphur Springs to Bozeman in the middle of the night." Ann and Rock were born in the hospital in Bozeman, Ann on November 1, the day Harry Truman was elected, and Paul remembered the doctor coming in to see the patient and sitting down on the bed and starting to cry, "tears rolling down his face…he was so shook up because Harry Truman had been elected President…it isn't often Mother had the doctor crying."

In 1952, Paul Ringling ran for the Montana State Legislature, serving one term. Then the next legislative session he ran successfully for the State Senate. From an interview with Paul:

In 1956 during the stock growers convention, the stock grower membership voted for a change in the assessment of livestock. It was introduced in the '57 Senate and almost all our legislation had to be introduced in the House, it was a tax related…passed the House which was supposed to be the wild, woolly bunch and controlled by the Democrats in '57 and came up to the '57 Senate, which was the first year the Democrats had controlled the Senate for several years…but anyway in and out of the Senate taxation committee and the damn stock grower members voted against it on the floor and in effect killed it in the Senate. Only two Stock Grower members in the Senate that voted for it, and that was Jack Brenner and I...Jack was a Republican from Beaverhead County and I was from Meagher County.

Paul also helped form the Cattlemen's Association in 1959, when the stock grower members in the Senate voted against a change in property tax on livestock—a change that all of the membership of the Stock Growers Association had supported.

When the Ringlings sold the ranch in White Sulphur Springs and purchased the Sheep Mountain Ranch at Springdale, Paul relinquished another senate run from Meagher County. He did run, unsuccessfully, for lieutenant governor in 1960. Paul Cannon was the Democratic candidate for governor.

The Farm Security Administration of the nation's Department of Agriculture got its start in the 1930s in order to help the farmers survive the Depression. The Standard Rural Rehabilitation Loan Program, provided credit, farm and home management planning and technical supervision. There were other programs that dealt with rural housing, rural business enterprises, rural water and waste disposal agencies, and price controls. The war brought new challenges and programs and by the late '50s, some of the agencies needed new management and purpose. Montana's department at Bozeman needed help. Through Senator Mike Mansfield, President John Kennedy asked Ringling to take on the office—to either "shape it up or close it." Ringling agreed to give it two years.

In two years, the office was reorganized, and the Commodity Stabilization Service became the Agricultural Stabilization and Conservation Service (ASCS) in 1961, with concentration on conservation. The new name reflected the agency's current missions.

SHEEP MOUNTAIN TO EKALAKA

In 1959, Paul, Althea, and the family pulled up stakes and moved to central Montana near Springdale in the Crazy Mountains. Paul Ringling raised Black Angus on a ranch on the south side of Sheep Mountain on range land where he said "every poisonous plant there ever was" grew, including "death camas, poison ivy, loco, larkspur, hemlock." He said, one day he was riding the range and came up over a hill to find twelve of his cattle, in rows, dead from eating poisonous plants.

In 1966, he bought a ranch he named The Ringling Ranch Limited Partnership in Carter County near Ekalaka, in the southeast corner of Montana, a ranch he describes as "just big enough." He still lived there as this book was written, at the age of ninety-three. "He wanted a deeded grass ranch without any public land," said Rock Ringling, his son.

A LIFE ON THE LAND

After working as a rancher most of his life, Paul observed that ranching has undergone enormous changes. One thing, however, has remained consistent: weather. "If you get the moisture when you need it, you can overcome a lot of things, but if Mother Nature turns her back on you, you're in big trouble." The other change is that the producer to retail spread is historically higher than it has ever been...so, as Paul pointed out, it is harder and harder for a producer to make it. "When my wife and I started ranching we owed a lot of money for quite a long time, but we could make enough to keep chipping away…but now, the price of a tractor or pickup or any tools, just tools, things that you use, if you have to buy them, they are well out of line with what we sell. You can relate it to how many steer calves or how many bushels of wheat or how many whatever, but it's way out of whack."

Still living on his own in his nineties, Paul observed that living in the country has made him more self-sufficient. "I had a really free life…when I was young, riding all over the country and doing hunting and fishing…you *thought* a little for yourself. I enjoy that environment…[M]aybe you tend to oversimplify, but you look at some people and wonder what they're doing for ham and eggs, and how they make it."

1. *Butte Miner*, 1924.
2. Brian Shovers, Paul Ringling Interview, Montana Historical Society, General Oral History Collection, OH 1982.
3. Caroline Patterson, Paul Ringling Interview, Helena, Montana, March 2013.
4. Shovers, Paul Ringling Interview.
5. Ibid.
6. Conversation with Lee Rostad.
7. Patterson, Paul Ringling Interview.

Acknowledgments

Thanks go to the Ringling family, who gave their memories and pictures to make the story; to Caroline Patterson; and especially to my niece, Susan Kasischke, who spent many hours researching in the dusty archives of Meagher County.

About the Author

Lee Rostad was born in Roundup, Montana, graduated from the University of Montana and spent a year in London as a Fulbright Scholar before marrying Phil Rostad, a rancher in the Musselshell Valley. She took her turn writing the social news for the weekly newspapers and took time from her ranching chores to write magazine articles. She is the author of the books *Honey Wine and Hunger Root, Fourteen Cents and Seven Green Apples, Grace Stone Coates: Her Life in Letters,* and *The House of Bair.*

In 1995, Lee received an Honorary Doctor of Letters from Rocky Mountain College and in 2001 received the Governor's Award in Humanities. She served on both the Montana Humanities Board and Montana Historical Society Board.